Texas Wanderlust

NUMBER: SIXTY-FIVE

The Centennial Series of the Association of Former Students, Texas A&M University

Emil Frederick "Dutch" Wurzbach, about 1860. A frontiersman and Rebel soldier, he suffered from a chronic case of Texas wanderlust.
Courtesy Douglas V. Meed

Texas Wanderlust

The Adventures of Dutch Wurzbach

DOUGLAS V. MEED

Texas A&M University Press
COLLEGE STATION

04 03 02 01 00 99 98 97 5 4 3 2 1

The paper used in this book meets the minimum requirements of the American National Standard for Permanence of Paper for Printed Library Materials, Z39.48-1984.

Binding materials have been chosen for durability.

Library of Congress Cataloging-in-Publication Data

Meed, Douglas V.
Texas wanderlust : the adventures of Dutch Wurzbach / by Douglas V. Meed
p. cm. — (The centennial series of the Association of Former Students, Texas A&M University ; no. 65)
Includes bibliographical references (p.) and index.
ISBN 0-89096-726-1 (alk. paper). — ISBN 0-89096-734-2 (pbk. : alk. paper)
1. Wurzbach, Emil Frederick. 2. German Americans—Texas—Biography. 3. Adventure and adventurers—Texas—Biography. 4. Frontier and pioneer life—Texas. 5. Texas—History—1846–1950. I. Title. II. Series.
F395.G3M44 1997
976.4'05'092—dc20 96-27122
[B] CIP

To Jeannine,

Michael, & Geoffrey

Contents

Illustrations

Preface

I first heard stories about my great-grandfather, Emil Frederick Wurzbach, from my father, Vincent D. Meed. As a young army lieutenant courting the young lady who was to become my mother, he had met the old warrior in 1921 at the family home on East Commerce Street in San Antonio.

On his trips from Fort Sam Houston to visit my mother, the young officer held many a conversation with the old soldier about frontier days in Texas, with Great-Grandfather occasionally throwing in a snide remark about the martial virtues of Yankee troops during the great War between the States. My father kept a discreet silence, although he was of Irish descent and one of his uncles had been killed with Meagher's Brigade at the bridge at Fredericksburg, and another was missing and never found after Cold Harbor.

The old Confederate, who had lost many a messmate all the way from Newtonia to Yellow Bayou, nevertheless formed a bond with this trim Yankee infantryman and regaled him with tales of the Old West until my mother, after an interval designed to keep callow suitors in suspense, made her appearance and the two departed for the social whirl of the post–World War I army.

It was almost two decades later, while I was a sixth grader shelving books after school at the San Antonio Public Library, for the princely sum of thirty-five cents an hour, that I stumbled upon my great-grandfather's memoirs.

The slim volume had been published in 1937 by the Yanaguana Society, a historical organization based in San Antonio. Great-Grandfather had dictated the memoirs to his daughter back in 1915, when he was seventy-eight years old. A local writer, Frederick C. Chabot, while preparing the genealogy of the Wurzbach family for his book, *With the Makers of San Antonio*, found the manuscript and had it published.

The evening I found the book, I fear that the library lost almost a dollar's worth of my time as, slouched down between the musty stacks, I followed my ancestor's adventures across the already fading trails of early Texas and the western frontier and into the bloody morass of battles in the war that pitted brother against brother and tore this nation apart.

In later years, I tracked down the events Great-Grandfather described so laconically, reassuring myself concerning the accuracy of times and places and verifying the names that my Great-Aunt Fanny had written down with phonetic accuracy if not grammatical exactitude. The tracking was not always easy.

Great-Grandfather, you see, was not a leader in the conventional sense. Unlike others in his family, he commanded no troops. Nor did he reign over vast tracts of land or blaze legislative trails in Austin or Washington, D.C. He was one of a unique breed of westerners who suffered from incurably itchy feet—what his German forebears had termed *der wanderlust.* Like some itinerant knight, he roamed the frontier seeking new adventures, driven by an insatiable desire to see what was over the next hill.

My relative battled Apaches and Comanches, hauled wagons over the desert, prospected for gold, broke horses, drove herds, and fought the hell out of the Yankee legions. He met with "Big Foot" Wallace, worked for Robert Neighbors, trailed with Albert Sidney Johnston, served under Gen. Dick Taylor, and luckily did not march with Gov. Henry A. Crabb. He charged the Yankee lines at Newtonia alongside a wild bunch of Cherokee Indians and Missouri guerrillas, and he helped to shatter a Union invasion at Mansfield under a general who was a French prince.

During the wild days of the western frontier, this intrepid adventurer, like many of his *compadres*, was present but went unnoticed in the annals of the day. Like many of his ilk who roamed freely across the West, he didn't give a damn for rank, titles, or outward signs of prestige. Men like him followed their own stars. Had he not dictated his memoirs, at his death he would have vanished without a trace—lost in time, as the yarn-spinning voices around the campfires thinned out with the years.

But fortunately there is this record. I have fleshed out Great-Grandfather's adventures with additional histories and testimonies of the times, trying to breathe life into one of those almost anonymous frontiersmen who rode across the wild expanses of this adolescent continent with one hand on the reins, one hand on a gun, and a wild song of freedom in their hearts.

By providing factual information, anecdotes, ideas, and encouragement, many people helped in the creation of this book. Special thanks go to Linda Wurzbach, Charlotte Wurzbach Brunson, Emily Wurzbach Mickler, Billie W. (Mrs. Reginald) Roberts, all of San Antonio, Texas; Robert Stonedale, Palacios, Texas; and Terry McCollister, El Paso, Texas.

Texas Wanderlust

CHAPTER I

On to Texas

On to Texas, on to Texas
Where the star in the blue field
Prophesies a new world.
—August Hoffman Von Fallersleben
"The Star of Texas"

The lookout, perched high in the rigging, shouted "Land ho!" In a fever of excitement, the young boy rushed to the rails of the sturdy barque *Andacia.* Staring far out across the short, choppy waves under a huge pale blue sky that seemed to go on forever, he could see only a brown stain on the horizon.

In his imaginative eight-year-old mind, Emil perhaps had expected to see painted Indian warriors dressed in barbaric splendor astride prancing wild ponies. Or perhaps he had hoped to see Carl, Prince of Solms-Braunfels, waving his plumed hat in greeting to the adventurous new arrivals. The brown stain he saw, however, was not very exciting. Excitement would come later.

Soon other members of the family joined Emil at the railing—his father, Jacob Daniel Wurzbach, a civil engineer now in the employ of the Adelsverein, the German Emigration Society; his mother, Louisa; and his ten-year-old brother, Charles Louis. At last—Texas! It had been 117 days of an exhausting voyage since they sailed out of Antwerp, and even longer since they left their comfortable home in Mannheim, in the Grand Dukedom of Baden.[1]

The family had sailed during the winter of 1845–46. A similar voyage was described by Ottile Fuchs Goeth, who wrote, "Our journey in the fall of the year was the worst imaginable time to sail. The food was wretched, the water barely drinkable, and we were seasick throughout most of the voyage. It was particularly rough in the North Sea, with its choppy green waves."[2]

Many of the vessels which transported those joining the German exodus to Texas in the first half of the nineteenth century were three-masted barques. Their two forward masts were square-rigged with billowing sails of limited maneuverability, designed to be pushed by the trade winds blowing astern. The third mast was rigged fore and aft with a wider latitude of movement, helping the craft change direction in coastal waters.

Typically, such barques were somewhat more than one hundred feet long and about thirty feet wide, had a shallow draft of not more than fifteen feet, and weighed 450 to 500 tons.[3] These were not the largest transatlantic vessels, but their smaller size and shallow draft were necessary if the ship was to ride over the oyster reefs and bars of shifting sand that partially blocked the few good Texas harbors. Such ships usually carried 150 to 200 passengers crowded in cold, drafty, smelly bunks.

Accommodations often consisted of two layers of bunks, each six feet square and two feet high, shared by five very crowded people. Headroom measured one and a half feet. Particularly in bad weather, nights became "horrible and terribly long," while breathing became "oppressive and difficult."[4] More affluent voyagers could book rooms sleeping only four persons, two above and two below, in a cramped cabin.[5]

The ship passengers' queasiness was diminished neither by the cramped quarters nor the culinary delights of the ship's mess. The food was the same for all—unappetizing at best. One passenger describes the total menu, varied slightly from day to day, as follows: bacon floating in peas, rice and salt meat, flour dumplings, beans, cabbage, barley, and cloudy water, "repeated week after week for the duration of the trip."[6] Menu aside, some of the passengers would "lose their appetite just looking at the cook's dirty clothing or his unwashed hands."[7] In bad weather, dining became chaos. When a large wave abruptly tilted the ship, plates of food, "forks, bowls, soup, meat, potatoes and gravy" cascaded down the mess table, covering the unfortunate diners in a meal transformed into garbage.[8]

In the excitement of seeing fabulous Texas upon the horizon, the Wurzbachs quickly forgot all these discomforts. The dangers and discomforts of ocean voyaging, however, were not yet behind them. Crossing the bar into Galveston Island harbor often was the most hazardous part of a trip. Many hopeful immigrants had met watery deaths as a ship carrying them became stranded on the harbor bar and was smashed by churning waves and vicious winds.

Galveston was a particularly treacherous place to land, since a ship could pass into the harbor only by threading through one of the narrow channels at each end of the island. These narrow inlets acted as funnels for large tidal waters that were compressed into driving currents either entering or leaving the bay. In March, landing was particularly dangerous, since the prevailing winds were still from the north. Blowing off the mainland, they would drive bay waters into the swiftly flowing waters of an incoming tidal current. Where wind-driven and tide-driven waters collided, a churning slash of white water ripped across the inlets and could drive a sailing ship onto a reef or knock it onto its beam ends, to be chopped to bits by wind and wave.

August Santleben, who landed in Galveston harbor in 1845, reports that one ship, stranded when it either missed the narrow channel or went aground on the bar about half a mile from shore, was broken to pieces, and all but thirty-five of its passengers drowned.[9]

The *Andacia*, however, was one of the lucky barques that landed without incident on the storm-blasted island of Galveston. The island itself was hardly the paradise imagined by the immigrants when they had decided to leave Germany for a new life in Texas. One voyager reported that many families landed on Galveston's sandy shores weakened from seasickness and malnutrition and covered with vermin. After being "huddled together in the holds, steerage, and on the decks of the ships like sheep . . . hundreds died soon after they landed. . . . The condition of affairs became frightful."[10]

In the face of the known hazards of an ocean voyage, two motives drove the exodus from Germany to Texas that began in the 1840s. One was widespread poverty that oppressed the countryside, as natural population increase overburdened the land with multitudinous younger sons and daughters who had little work and few prospects of getting more. In the cities, the economic future looked just as gloomy. Germany had not yet fully entered the industrial age. Unless one was the eldest son of a guild member, the crafts were difficult to enter; and wages, even for skilled craftsmen, were abysmally low. Farm produce brought only miserable returns for long and hard labor. Taxes, however, were high and going higher. Young people found it increasingly difficult to marry and start families of their own.

Political unrest was growing, not only among the impoverished but also among educated middle-class Germans. Inspired by the American and French revolutions and the writings of Enlightenment political philosophers, the latter group became increasingly restive supporting the courtly pomposities of various dukes, margraves, princes, counts, and other minor aristocrats who reigned over the patchwork German states.

Jacob Wurzbach was among those intellectuals who resented the growing restrictions on free speech and the political subservience imposed by feudal German lords. But, according to Great-Grandfather, Jacob most feared the growing influence of Prussia and the rampant militarism of the German states. "When," said Jacob, "on a narrow sidewalk, a free citizen must step into the gutter to allow a uniformed officer, clanking with medals and saber, to pass, then it is time to seek freedom in a different land."[11]

Hatred of the military was in keeping with Wurzbach family tradition. It went back as far as the Thirty Years War that had ravaged Germany during the seventeenth century. In that bloody time, the Wurzbach Von Tannenburgs had held a barony on the Prussian marches (borders). When religious disputes tore Germany apart during those grim three decades of civil war, one of the two Wurzbach Von Tannenburg brothers espoused the Protestant cause, the other the Catholic.

In that particular instance, the Catholic side won out, and the Protestant side of the family, stripped of its titles, fled to asylum in the city of Mannheim, on the Rhine River in the state of Baden.[12] It was from these refugees that Emil and his family descended. For almost two hundred years, the Wurzbachs (*Von Tannenburg* was dropped from the family name) became teachers, engineers, and ministers in the more tolerant environment of southeastern Germany. But hatred of war, militarism, and Prussian harshness remained strongly embedded in the family psyche.

In 1846, the sparks of revolution, which two years later were to burst into a flame of revolt that swept across Europe, were creating great unease among the comfortable burghers and titled rulers of the German states. The German nobility was not unaware of the discontent rising among both peasants and members of the middle class. In 1842, a group of twenty-one nobles formed an association that, "mindful of the increasing excess of population and the poverty growing therefrom, particularly among the lower classes of people, made it their object to redress this evil by regulating the already considerable emigration."[13] The nobles did not mention that emigration also was a convenient way to get rid of dissident intellectuals.

The group organized what was to become the Society for the Protection of German Immigrants in Texas, known generally as the Adelsverein. The organization directed German immigrants to Texas and pledged funds to support them until they reaped their first harvest and so could repay the society.

The noblemen, whose skills did not extend to sound business practices, soon acquired the right to settle a massive tract of land in

West Texas called the Fisher-Miller Grant, exceeding three million acres. In January, 1844, Carl, Prince of Solms-Braunfels, was appointed commissioner-general of the association; he soon boarded ship to Texas to found the first settlement.

The grant entitled each family to 320 acres upon settling the land, cultivating fifteen acres, and building a house. To land-starved Germans, Texas sounded like the promised land. The Adelsverein also promised that, after landing in Texas, immigrants would be provided wagons to transport their families and belongings to the grant site, a house would be built for them, and grain and farming implements would be provided. With these considerations, it is no wonder that Germans by the thousands signed up to immigrate to this fabulous country that—they were told—had a climate like that of Sicily, with no winter; had soil that needed no fertilizer; and had a democratic government that would welcome them.[14] The reality, however, was to prove crushingly different.

Two conditions frustrated the naïve aspirations of the new settlers. First, the Adelsverein, perhaps well-intentioned but fiscally inept, had insufficient funds to fulfill its promises; it was bankrupt in 1847. Second, by mid-April, 1846, United States regulars had clashed with Mexican forces in South Texas, and by early May the two countries were at war.

It was a double-barreled disaster for the German families. Many who, for lack of funds, had been stranded earlier on the beaches of Galveston now were left immobile because almost all mules, oxen, horse teams, and wagons were seized by the U.S. Army, which was preparing to move a force of regulars, volunteers, and militia from South Texas to the Rio Grande for a planned invasion of Mexico.

One traveler, Alwin H. Sörgel, a former bookstore owner and a keen observer who arrived in Galveston on February 3, 1846, found "seven hundred to eight hundred immigrants" piled into "three large wooden buildings."[15] There, in one of the "most unhealthy places in Texas," sickness broke out, there was a lack of wood and water, and mosquitoes and fever were endemic; most of the families were destitute.[16]

Prince Carl of Solms-Braunfels. He led the idealistic German pioneers to their new homes in Texas. Courtesy Archives Division, Texas State Library, Austin

Still more families landed at the crowded port and were crammed into what was becoming a deadly slum. From the middle of October, 1845, through April, 1846, thirty-six ships, loaded with more than 5,200 German immigrants, disembarked at the Galveston dock. But if conditions were bad, they could get worse; and they did. Emil remembered a flood at Galveston when "my father put us on the roof of our house and began to tie the rafters together to keep the house from coming to pieces."[17] Laconically he reported, "My mother did not like to live in Galveston."[18]

Sometime in 1846, the little family secured passage on a small steamer that carried them 125 miles down the Texas coast to the hurricane-battered port of Indian Point, on Lavaca Bay.[19] That trip, too, was not without its dangers. In addition to the shoals and sandbars, unscrupulous skippers of coastal vessels sometimes ran their boats aground, providing an excuse to heave the passengers' belongings overboard so as to "lighten ship." Cronies lurking ashore then would rush into the shallow waters and claim the goods as salvage. Other skippers were said to wreck their ships to collect maritime insurance. Soon no insurance company would write a policy for ships and goods sailing to Indian Point.[20] But the Wurzbach family survived the trip without incident.

Arriving at Indian Point, passengers disembarked onto a spindly wharf that stretched 250 feet out into the shallow waters. There the steamer unloaded. Upon reaching land, they encountered a horror that, by comparison, made Galveston seem pleasant. At an improvised settlement named Carlshafen by the not-so-modest Carl, Prince of Solms-Braunfels, more than two thousand settlers were huddled in tents. There, Sörgel reported, "eighteen individuals die daily."[21]

Dr. Ferdinand Roemer, a renowned paleontologist who made extensive studies of the new land at first hand, described their plight: "About 3,000 of the poor immigrants lay crowded on the sandy coast, without an adequate water supply or fuel, living in sod houses or tents which afforded no protection against the rain nor against the hot rays of the sun."[22] In addition, "malaria, bilious fever and dysentery soon became general and mortality increased with alarming rapidity."[23]

Roemer sadly reported, "It is certain that in the few summer months of the year 1846 more than one thousand out of 4,000 German immigrants . . . died and not more than one thousand two hundred actually settled upon the land secured by the Verein."[24]

Many of the young married men in the settlement joined the

American army, because, as Alwin Sörgel recounted, "it is better to fight the Mexicans man to man than be a defenseless victim of the poisonous and creeping illnesses and the millions of mosquitos."[25]

This New World version of the Black Hole of Calcutta had little appeal for the Wurzbach family. After great effort and no little expenditure of funds, a dozen teams of oxen finally were procured. Jacob was elected leader of a small band of immigrants who decided to push inland to the new German settlement at Fredericksburg, almost two hundred miles to the north.[26]

A number of small way stations along the route had been founded the previous year by a prudent Prince Carl, who realized that wagons hauled by oxen could make little more than ten miles a day, at best, over primitive roads which were little more than tracks or wheel ruts left by the few travelers who had passed by at an earlier date.

In this new land, there were no bridges across the many streams, arroyos, and rivers that crisscrossed South and Central Texas. At each water barrier, wagon trains stopped while scouts searched for a ford. Often, particularly after a rainstorm, when even dry arroyos became torrential streams, no ford could be found where oxen could pull heavily laden wagons across the churning waters. Then camp was made, and wagons were circled as protection against Indian attack. The oxen were hobbled and allowed to graze. Boys and girls took wooden buckets to the river and hauled water, while the women washed and prepared meals. The men, armed with axes and saws, searched for suitable trees or driftwood out of which to construct rafts.

Rafting put a terrible strain on the travelers. Everything had to be laboriously unloaded from the wagons, reloaded on the flimsy rafts, and hauled across the water. The animals swam and the wagons were rafted across. After reloading the wagons and hitching up the draft animals, the exhausted travelers continued their journey along the dusty trails until they reached the next flooded stream, where the entire tiresome procedure had to be repeated. Sometimes the waters were so turbulent that a wagon train would be forced to camp for weeks, until the raging stream subsided.

Under the best of conditions, traveling the 150 miles to New Braunfels, the first large settlement along the route, could take several weeks by slow-moving oxen. Along the trail, epidemics originating in the unhealthy coastal areas took a heavy toll on the settlers.

Alwin Sörgel, who made the trek, wrote, "I am reluctant to describe the misery of those who fell sick and who died without any help or care on that journey. . . . Many times wolves and vultures shared their corpses. A husband took his ailing wife off the wagon, to be relieved of caring for her."[27] Abandoned, the woman was left on the trail to die a lonely death shared only by birds and beasts of prey that hovered in hungry vigil.

Death on the trail, however, was not without its ironies. Soon the lout who left his wife to die fell ill himself and became too weak to travel. With the same measure of indifference, his fellow trekkers took him from his wagon and laid him by the trail to suffer the same fate as his wife. Unlike her, he was not mourned.[28]

Entire families were wiped out, and the immigrant trail from Indian Point to New Braunfels became a trail of tears. Scores of wooden crosses marked the graves of forlorn seekers after a better life.[29]

Suffering from malnutrition, exposure, and the back-wrenching work necessary to keep the wagons rolling, many men died, leaving a large number of bereft widows and orphans, according to Viktor Bracht, a native of Düsseldorf and an employee of the Adelsverein.[30] Some who survived fever, diarrhea, and exposure were crushed in spirit by their travail. Brokenhearted over the deaths of loved ones, they returned to Germany discouraged and impoverished, with only their shattered dreams to show for their year of Texas misery.

But most forged on. Some, like young Emil, perhaps were too young to appreciate the difficulties of the journey or at an early age developed a frontiersman's callousness to hardship. Remembering the trip almost seven decades later, Emil said, "We had a long trip to make with ox teams. I do not remember anything special happening until we got near New Braunfels. There one man's wife died the night we stopped at New Braunfels, and when we crossed the river the next morning, the man threw his dead wife in the river, left her to float off down the river."[31]

Emil's report that "we had one little fight with the Indians between New Braunfels and Fredericksburg, which did not amount to much," perhaps describes an event that was, after all that had gone before, anticlimactic.[32]

New Braunfels was a welcome haven for the weary travelers. The little town had been founded on March 21, 1845, by Prince Carl, who had bought a tract of land to serve as a way station along the route to the big Fisher-Miller land grant. Roemer commented, "In all of Western Texas no more beautiful and suitable spot could have been chosen for a settlement."[33] The town was situated on a small plain bounded to the south by gentle hills; to the east ran the pure, clear waters of the Guadalupe River; north and west were bounded by Comal Creek. Nearby hills were covered with cedars and juniper trees, and the flat nearby plains were covered with grass that provided forage for animals. Inspired by the beauty of the surroundings, the prince sentimentally named the town after Braunfels, the seat of his ancestral home. Before the end of 1845, 150 houses had been built and occupied by the industrious *herrenvolk*.[34]

Early life in the German settlements, however, was difficult, as Rosa Von Roeder Kleberg, a young bride and the daughter of a well-to-do landholder in Marienmunster, observed. She and her sister, to help support the family, took sewing lessons and made clothes to be sold in a local store. "We were all unused to that kind of work . . . ," she said, perhaps with an aristocrat's disdain; but, "when required by necessity, one learns to do what one has never done before." To raise additional funds, Rosa sold some "fine linen table cloth" brought from Germany.[35]

There were some compensations. The family piano, badly damaged in a shipwreck off the coast of Galveston Island, was saved and repaired, and while Rosa played, young people in the neighborhood danced. "Our home," she said, "was the meeting place of many young, educated Germans who . . . hoped to find in Texas the land of freedom." Rosa remembered when "Prince Solms-Braunfels came to our house one day. . . . He impressed me as a conceited fool."[36]

Others had it much worse. Caroline Von Hinueber, the daughter of a bookkeeper from the Duchy of Oldenburg, arrived in Texas when she was eleven or twelve years of age. Her first house "was a miserable little hut covered with straw." She recalled, "We suffered a great deal in the winter. My father had tried to build a chimney and fireplace out of logs and clay, but we were afraid to light a fire because of the extreme combustibility of our dwelling. So we had to shiver. Our shoes gave out, and we had to go barefoot in the winter. . . . My mother slept on a deerskin, without a pillow, on the floor. . . . We had very little to eat. We ate nothing but corn bread at first."[37]

Amid all this hardship and privation, there was one overriding advantage for young ladies. Women of marriageable age were very scarce on the frontier. Emma Murck Altgelt, who at age twenty arrived in Galveston, remembered: "As soon as we landed . . . Germans rushed aboard ship . . . to find out if there were any girls aboard, at that time a rare article." Some of the unattached women, Emma reported, found partners even before they left the ship. This situation stood in contrast to that in the homeland, where many could not afford to marry because of lack of jobs and opportunity.[38]

On a hilltop at New Braunfels, the prince built a log stockade as protection against attack by the swarms of Comanches who passed through the area. There he placed 4- and 6-pounder cannons, "rifles, guns and ammunition of every sort. At sunrise and sunset we always fired a cannon, which resounded far into the mountains and gave them (the Indians) an understanding of what to expect in case they tried to attack," he wrote.[39] The proud prince named his fortress "Sophienburg" in honor of the "Lady to whom I devoted my heart," Lady Sophia, widowed Princess of Salm-Salm, born Princess of Lowenstein-Wertheim-Rosenberg-Rochefort.[40]

In July, 1844, Prince Carl, young (he was thirty-three years old), slender, handsome, with aquiline features and a stylishly wide curling mustache, arrived in Galveston to take up his duties as head of the Adelsverein. With a few companions, he journeyed through much of South and Central Texas, only to realize that the Fisher-Miller Grant, upon which, sight unseen, the Adelsverein had purchased the right to settle, was unsuitable for the horde of incoming immigrants. Not only was it three hundred miles from the Gulf Coast ports, but also it was more than one hundred miles from the towns of San Antonio and Austin, the only settlements where supplies could be obtained.

Most important, the grant was located in country dominated by the fierce Comanche Indians, for whom raiding, looting, and sneak attacks were a treasured way of life. While settlers just might be able to raise a crop on the Fisher-Miller Grant, they were more likely to get scalped by those ubiquitous raiders of the plains. In frustration, the prince later wrote that Fisher (the entrepreneur who had negotiated with the Adelsverein) was not worth "the cord it would take to hang him and Miller."[41]

After coming to these realizations, the prince purchased land around New Braunfels. Each arriving settler was given a town lot and a ten-acre tract to be occupied until the Fisher-Miller land could be surveyed and made safe for settlement. In mid-May, 1845, less than two months after founding New Braunfels, the prince, considering his work done, departed for Germany, never to return to Texas.

His successor, Baron Ottfried Hans Von Meusebach, inherited the financial mess created by the Adelsverein. That organization may have been successful in producing starry-eyed German immigrants, but it was totally incapable of securing the funds needed to support them upon their arrival in the new land. Arriving in Texas during the spring of 1845, the baron, who had both business acumen and administrative ability, settled the difficult financial situation as well as could be expected. Meusebach gave up his title shortly after arriving in Texas, stating cynically but correctly, "Names mean nothing to Americans. Gold and votes carry importance."[42]

With a flood of new families scheduled to arrive in the fall, Meusebach quickly realized that even the industrious burghers of

New Braunfels could not accommodate all the new settlers. Scouting through the country along the Llano and Pedernales rivers, some seventy-five miles northwest of New Braunfels, Meusebach located a ten-thousand-acre tract with good water and ample timber, that seemed suitable for settlement. With his remaining funds he purchased the tract, surveyed it, and readied it for the coming influx of immigrants. He named the new town Fredericksburg, to honor one of the more prominent members of the Adelsverein, Prince Frederick of Prussia.

In addition to making sense of the muddled legal and financial affairs of the Adelsverein and purchasing needed land, Meusebach attended to a few other matters. He took one look at the militia raised by Prince Carl to safeguard the colonists and demanded an immediate change of uniform. The men, wearing "hats bedecked with cockade of rooster feathers, gauntlet gloves and long clanking sabres," although tough and dedicated guardians, were the laughing stock of the equally tough but unpretentious and irreverent Texas Ranger forces who defended the Anglo settlements.[43]

Meanwhile, those immigrants who had made it up from the coast were determined to continue onward. The first train of twenty wagons and two two-wheeled carts left New Braunfels for Fredericksburg on April 23, 1846, with 120 courageous pioneers. In later years, Pastor Louis Cachand described the trip to his daughter, stating, "Most of the people had some kind of fever or scurvy from poor food. . . . It rained all the time . . . with oxcarts sticking in the mud . . . wet and miserable. . . . Provisions were scarce."[44] After sixteen days of hard going over land rising into a series of rolling hills with hard limestone ridges, soils ranging from waxy black to sandy loam, the immigrant train reached the site of the new settlement on May 8. In June another wagon train arrived.

The Wurzbachs, after a short rest in New Braunfels, made the trek to Fredericksburg in late fall, just in time to encounter a wave of fever, dysentery, and spinal meningitis that swept the fledging community, killing ninety-four people.[45] But by the end of the year, five hundred hard-working Germans were clearing brush, trees, and stumps; erecting log houses with the walls chinked with mud; planting crops; and creating homes in the wilderness.

In January, 1847, the peripatetic paleontologist, Dr. Ferdinand Roemer, left New Braunfels. Braving an icy "norther," he traveled through the undulating hills to arrive at Fredericksburg on January 20. Six miles from the banks of the narrow but swiftly flowing Pedernales River, lined with gnarled post oaks and prolific pecan trees, Roemer found the settlement. Surrounded by a vast unexplored wilderness, miles from any town where supplies could be purchased and deep in the heart of Comanche territory, it had a drab and forlorn look. Standing guard over its fifty log houses and temporary huts was a palisade of posts dug into the ground, with a small cannon sited by the gate.[46]

Shortly after Romer's arrival Meusebach departed for Comanche country on a peace mission. Meusebach earlier had made friends with the nearby tribe of Waco Indians who, constantly raided by the Comanches, may have welcomed the hardy settlers whose firearms might well discourage their ancient foes. On January 22, 1847, accompanied by a party of twenty militia and several surveyors, he set out to negotiate with the Comanches. Since Jacob Wurzbach, a civil engineer, at one time was employed by the Adelsverein and was in Fredericksburg at that time, it is possible that he was included in the party.[47]

Meusebach planned to confer with the Penatekas, the deadliest clan of raiders on the North American continent. It was an idea that sent shivers through the Texan community, for the Comanches' hatred of Texans and Mexicans was the pathological result of mutual betrayals and multiple atrocities committed by all sides. Either mad or inspired, Meusebach believed that he could strike a deal with those fierce warriors.

Moving north into the Fisher-Miller Grant across the Llano River and approaching the San Saba River, deep in the heart of Comanche Country, Meusebach's small party was startled by the sudden appearance of a band of mounted warriors. The confrontation was tense, with Comanche fingers poised on bowstrings and lances clenched at the ready, while the Germans nervously fingered triggers and sword hilts.

Meusebach, whose broad, friendly features emerged from a full set of flowing whiskers, soon eased the tension with smiling, hearty greetings. He was able to convince the Indians that he came in peace. Later he rode into their camp, fired his rifle into the air, and, with the weapon thus unloaded, dismounted to talk and distribute gifts to the chiefs. More than two hundred Comanches in full festive regalia paraded before him, while a chief draped him in a buffalo robe.[48]

After the traditional peace pipe had been puffed around a circle of Germans and Comanches and preliminary discussions had been held, the two sides agreed to meet again the following day.

Meanwhile, back in New Braunfels, Robert Simpson Neighbors, a former major in the army of the Republic of Texas and a notable frontiersman, had been sent by the governor of Texas to dissuade Meusebach from venturing into Comanche territory. Finding that the baron already had departed, Neighbors, with a few companions (including the always adventuresome Dr. Roemer), set out in pursuit. On February 10, they arrived at Meusebach's camp; and Neighbors, one of the few Texans who were on good terms with the tribesmen, offered his assistance in negotiating with the Penatekas.

It was a rare time on the frontier, because a genuine bond seems to have been created linking Meusebach, Neighbors, and the Comanche chiefs Old Owl, Santa Anna, and Buffalo Hump. Far into the cool nights, under a canopy of countless stars, they sat around the campfires singing. First the Germans sang, then the Comanches chanted. *Lieder* and drinking songs mingled with hymns to the Great Spirit. It was a time that showed what could, but rarely did, exist—a time when white and red men came together as friends.[49]

While Meusebach's good will, peaceful intentions, and gifts undoubtedly won over the "Lords of the Plains," the presence of Neighbors, a known friend of the Comanches, certainly contributed toward cementing ties of respect and friendship among those

Robert Simpson Neighbors and his wife, Elizabeth Ann. As a young boy Dutch worked on the ranch of this famous frontiersman. Courtesy Center for American History, University of Texas at Austin

men of very different worlds. An agreement was reached. The Comanches permitted the Germans to establish a settlement on the Llano River; in return for this permission, the Comanches would receive presents at a March meeting in Fredericksburg. In the future, when Germans and Comanches met, they agreed, they would meet as friends.

While Comanches and Germans were on friendly terms on the San Saba, back in Fredericksburg, stealthy Comanches were watching the German community with a sharp eye out for treachery. They scanned the German settlers from vantage points on the surrounding hills, and at night their signal fires bathed the summits in eerie light.

Emil, his older brother Charles, and the other children at first were frightened by these mysterious fires in the night. But their fears turned into astonishment when an ingenious German mother told the children that the fires were set by the Easter Rabbit, who was boiling eggs in great cauldrons on the hilltops. Then, the mother said, the Easter Rabbit would dye the eggs with the beautiful colors of the wildflowers that sprang up in the Hill Country during the early spring. The colorful eggs, she said, would be given to the *kinder* during a great pageant which would be held at Easter. To the delight of the children, from that time on, they always were given colored hard-boiled eggs every Easter Sunday.[50]

On March 2, 1847, Comanches and Germans met again in Fredericksburg. They signed a treaty according to which, in exchange for three thousand dollars in presents, the Texas Hill Country and three million acres of the Fisher-Miller Grant were opened up for settlement. It was one of the very few treaties made between white men and red that never was shattered by either side.

It is very likely that, at this time, Jacob Wurzbach introduced his youngest son to the burly Major Neighbors. The major grasped the boy's small hand in his meaty paw and said, "Howdy, Dutch." From then on, for more than eighty years, Emil Frederick was known to family and friends as "Dutch."[51]

With the treaty signed, Germans by the hundreds began to homestead small farms and ranches throughout the rolling hill country. At last, after hunger, disease, exhaustion, and, all too often, the death of loved ones, the German wanderers had achieved their dream. In the words of their revered poet Johann Wolfgang Goethe, they at last were able to "stand on a free earth, among a people free."[52]

CHAPTER 2

A-Wandering

There's sunshine in the heart of me,
My blood sings in the breeze;
The mountains are a part of me,
I'm fellow to the trees.
My golden youth I'm squandering,
Sun-libertine am I;
A-wandering, a-wandering.
—Robert Service

For Dutch and Charles, who shared an adventurous and mischievous nature, living in Fredericksburg during the latter part of 1846 and the first half of 1847 resembled a Huckleberry Finn idyll. In his old age, Dutch gleefully recounted how he and Charles often would water their father's horses in a nearby creek. There they would strip off their clothes, dredge up red and black mud, and paint their bodies and faces like Indians. Hiding in the brush, the two lads would wait patiently for other boys to bring horses to the stream. Then, whooping and howling war cries, they would leap out and give their pals a good scare.[1] Somehow the two acquired a bevy of baby bears, which they trained to "fight the other boys." When not terrorizing their schoolmates, they spent hours visiting nearby Indian encampments, "which was great fun."[2]

This warm, happy interlude, however, was crushed by sorrow when their beloved mother, Louisa, suddenly became ill and died. The formerly happy family members never could overcome their grief, and perhaps that was the cause of an estrangement between father and sons that occurred soon after.

After his wife's death, Jacob and his two sons moved to Austin, where he enrolled the boys in school. "I did not learn much," Dutch confessed. Relations between the boys and Jacob must have been worsening, because Dutch recalled a "good whipping" he received for speaking English to a German who called upon his father.[3]

Late in the fall of 1847, Major Neighbors called upon the elder Wurzbach and must have spent considerable time talking with Dutch. The big frontiersman must have sensed the boy's unhappiness, for, before he left, he "persuaded" Jacob to let Dutch come to live with him on his farm on Salado Creek near San Antonio.[4]

With his father's approval, Dutch packed his few belongings and, bidding a sad farewell to Charles, left with the major for the farm. He was to be happy there, not surprisingly, for Robert Simpson Neighbors was one of the best-liked men in the state. He also was one of the most distinguished public servants and frontiersmen that Texas ever produced. Sadly, this man who accomplished so much is almost forgotten now, while many frontier badmen, such as John Wesley Hardin and Sam Bass, are household names to Texas history buffs.

Neighbors, a Virginian, came to the state during the Texans' revolution against Mexico. Serving as an officer in the Army of the Republic, he was captured in 1840 and held in a Mexican prison for almost four years. After returning to Texas, he began a distinguished career as an Indian agent for the state, subsequently, as we have seen, helping Meusebach secure his treaty with the Comanches.

In 1849, Neighbors led a small expedition, accompanied by famed Texas Ranger Capt. John Salmon "Rip" Ford and the Comanches' crafty Chief Buffalo Hump, to pioneer a practical wagon route from East and Central Texas across mountains and desert to a western terminus at El Paso. In 1850 he laid out and organized El Paso County, which was to remain the westernmost outpost of Texas.

Elected to the legislature, the major sponsored the creation of reservations on Texas state land to protect those Comanches who hoped to abandon their lives of raiding and live peacefully. The reservations, however, were failures, and Neighbors later moved his Indian charges to a federal reservation in Oklahoma. Although his life constantly was threatened by frontier thugs who hated him for championing Indian rights, Neighbors continued to fight for the cause of the tribesmen. Doing so eventually cost him his life. On September 14, 1859, he was shot from behind and killed at Fort Belknap, allegedly because of remarks he made criticizing a white man for murdering an Indian.[5] One of his grieving friends termed him "as gallant a knight as any who ever balanced a lance or drew a broadsword in behalf of the oppressed."[6]

This tragedy was in the far future, however, when young Dutch arrived at the farm. There, he became fast friends with another ward of Neighbors', a fourteen-year-old Mexican boy named Ignacio Serna, whom the major had rescued from the Comanches and whom he supported and educated. With two other hired hands, they "had a good time milking the cows and taking care of the horses and hogs and hunting up cattle. We would go fishing at night and hunting for bees in the daytime," Dutch recalled.[7]

The daredevil in Dutch, which would involve him in no end of narrow escapes in the future, got him into trouble one morning when he was rounding up calves. "I lay down in the tall grass and bleated like a calf until the wolves came up to within five or six feet of me, then I would jump up and throw rocks at them." But one morning there were three big "looper" wolves, and they were going to "jump at me." Dutch—who, like most frontiersmen, believed that discretion was always the better part of valor—ran for a tree and, as he said, stayed there for "a long time before they went away."[8]

With Neighbors away on Indian business most of the time, the job of maintaining discipline at the farm fell to the major's sister, Mary. With her own family to take care of, her patience with the ten-year-old hell-raiser may have been limited, or perhaps Dutch simply was too much for anyone to handle. In any event, he recounted, "I did not stay long with Major Neighbors because his sister wanted to whip me and I ran away to San Antonio."[9]

Straggling into San Antonio with no money and no place to stay, he was befriended by a young German woman, Mrs. Mary Guenther, who ran a boarding house on Main (now Commerce) Street. Probably the "kind" lady and Dutch compared notes about their respective voyages from Germany. She may have recalled how her ship had to maneuver outside Galveston for ten days, until a southerly wind blew enough water into the bay to enable it to cross the treacherous harbor bar.

The day after Dutch arrived in town, Mary, after cleaning his clothes and filling him up with some stick-to-your-ribs German cooking, took the feisty youngster to a nearby saddlery, where he could learn a useful trade.[10] After a few days of cutting leather, hammering nails, and stitching rawhide, however, he decided that the life of a saddle maker was not for him.

Like many another young runaway, when things got tough, Dutch headed back to his father's house. The trip from San Antonio to Austin was seventy miles, over what could hardly be called a road. Although the boy obviously was too poor to elicit an attack by one of the many highwaymen who infested the area, there were always roaming bands of Comanches or Kiowas who would have delighted in capturing a strong ten-year-old for a life of camp slavery. While Dutch was enterprising, resolute, and tough for his age, he was also exceedingly lucky; more than seven years later, in September, 1855, a young man was murdered by Indian raiders on the outskirts of San Antonio.[11]

Dutch, unfazed by the danger, started his trek across the almost deserted country, stopping, perhaps, for a glass of well water at the communities of New Braunfels, York Creek, and San Marcos; sleeping alongside the trail; and shivering throughout the cold nights, until, in the spring of 1848, footsore and weary, he arrived at his father's doorstep.[12]

He found his father saddened, homesick, and discouraged. By 1849, Jacob, announcing that he had given up, sold the property he had acquired in Austin. He and his two sons, he said, would return to Germany. But first they must get Charles, who also had left home and was living on a ranch near Fort Graham, on the Brazos River, more than a hundred miles to the north. That country was still largely under the control of the Comanche raiders.

Father and son packed supplies and saddled up; with Jacob riding a fine mare and Dutch on a mule, the duo struck out across what was still a no-man's-land of frontier Texas. After days in the saddle and nights in bedrolls under the stars, the two got within eighteen miles of Fort Graham, not too far from the present city of Waco, when Jacob called a halt and announced that they would camp for the night.

Having gathered wood, Jacob made a small campfire to cook the evening meal. Serene in their little camp, the older man prepared to relax after a hard day in the saddle. Dutch, however, was not so sanguine. After spending so much time with Indians, as well as living an outdoors life, he perhaps had developed a frontiersman's exquisite sensitivity to his surroundings. As Dutch recounted the subsequent events in his memoirs, what followed must have happened somewhat like this:

"*Vater*," Dutch murmured, "I don't like this place. I think there are Indians close by." In Texas in the 1840s, this statement was a sure conversation-stopper. "Listen. Every few moments your mare is snorting and twisting her head. My mule is not eating. It's not right."

To Jacob's credit, he did not dismiss Dutch's forebodings as merely the fears of a young boy. "Saddle your mule, son. Quietly," Jacob muttered, handing the boy his big pistol. "I'm going to make some coffee," he announced, probably in a voice a little bit louder than normal. While Jacob made a big production of noisily banging tin coffee cups and rustling around the fire, Dutch furtively slipped into the enveloping darkness and saddled the mule.

"Now," Jacob muttered, "put the bridle on my horse and bring me the reins." This done, Dutch led the mare to his father's side and handed him the reins. With cold sweat soaking their clothes even in the chill of the evening, father and son, ears straining for the slightest unnatural sound, waited. Moving slowly, Jacob inched toward the shotgun lying beside his bedroll. "Mount up, son," he whispered.

As Dutch carefully climbed up on the mule's back, an eerie silence fell over the camp. Suddenly a soul-searing yell shattered the quiet, and a shadowy band of Indians broke from a patch of chaparral. Brandishing scalping knives and war clubs, they charged the camp. The animals panicked. Jacob's mare reared, tore the reins from its owner's hands, and, neighing in terror, ran off into the night. The mule gave a few wild bucks, but Dutch held onto his saddle as Jacob screamed, "Ride off, son! Ride off!" But Dutch refused to leave his father, and, with Jacob blasting away with his shotgun and Dutch firing the big pistol, the two beat a fighting retreat into the darkness.

At a rather tender age even for the Texas frontier, eleven-year-old Dutch had fired his first shot in anger at a band of Indian raiders. It would not be the last time he exchanged gunfire with hostile Indians.[13]

These Indians, in the face of the gunfire, stayed their pursuit and satisfied themselves with catching the mare and looting the campsite. Groping about in the darkness, Jacob and Dutch finally found the trail to Fort Graham and, with the father clutching the mule's withers, the ungainly threesome stumbled and cursed their way through the night. Shortly after dawn they reached the Brazos River. In the dim light, they could see the outlines of the little fort nestled on the east bank. Fort Graham had been established only a few months earlier, in the spring of 1849, by the Second Dragoon Regiment of the U.S. Army.

Wading the shallow Brazos, father and son stumbled into the fort and reported the attack to the commanding officer. Quickly, with bugle blasts echoing across the Hill Country, a detail of dragoons swung into the saddle and headed south to pick up the trail of the raiders. As all too often happened, however, the trail faded out, and the marauders escaped.

During their brief stay at Fort Graham, Dutch met many junior officers who later would become famous. Stationed there were 1st Lt. Richard Herron Anderson and Capt. William Joseph Hardee, both of whom later became lieutenant generals in the Army of the Confederacy.

Life at Fort Graham, as at many a forlorn and isolated outpost on the frontier, was characterized by loneliness, stark living conditions, and hard monotonous duty. The strain often caused human emotions to explode into violence. When Bvt. Lt. Col. William Grigsby Freeman made an inspection of the fort in September, 1853, Lt. Anderson was in command. The post commander, Maj. Ripley A. Arnold, had been shot and killed on September 6, after an argument with the post's assistant surgeon, Josephus M. Steiner, who was being held in civil custody.

Some of the garrison's officers deemed Arnold a "martinet and hypocrite" who was defrauding the government by selling off good horses and replacing them with inferior stock. Others said he was an honorable and able officer. Steiner, after several courts-martial and trials, was cashiered for the killing and for fleeing to escape prosecution.[14]

Desertions were not infrequent, and punishment was not always mild. One recaptured miscreant received "fifty lashes . . . well laid on with rawhide" and was confined for the remainder of his enlistment with "ball and chain" attached to his leg.

The garrison, according to one observer, was a "refuge of drunkards, felons, failures and social misfits." Amid the normal boredom, there were some lively moments, for, if the loneliness didn't always induce grudge fights, it often encouraged bizarre behavior. During the 1850s, Capt. W. H. Saunders took a desperately needed leave to Austin. After leaving one of the grog mills there, he engaged in behavior leading to his being court-martialed: "Exposing in the most degrading manner in a public alley in the town of Austin, Texas, the privacy of his person, by taking down his pantaloons and assuming the usual stooped posture for the performance of an office of nature." There were also charges of embezzlement of funds and removal of public letters.[15]

After resting up at the fort, Jacob bought a horse from a nearby trader, and he and Dutch rode fifteen miles northwest along the Brazos River until they reached the farm of Sam Corothers, where they found Charles working as a farmhand. The older boy, as headstrong as his younger brother, refused to leave. Texas, he said, was now his home, and he refused to return to Germany.[16] Sadly, Jacob allowed Charles his decision. Bidding the boy an emotional farewell, he and Dutch took the long trail south to Indian Point, from whence, defeated, they intended to book passage back to Germany.

Fate, however, intervened. As the pair arrived at Indian Point, terrible winds swept over the area. Rain poured down in sheets so dense that Jacob and Dutch could hardly see ten yards in front of them; the almost horizontally driven raindrops whipped their faces like flying gravel. The wind smashed rooftops, and the surging tidal waters tore small boats from their moorings and drove them ashore, bottoms ripped. Jacob, head in hands, shrugged and said, "The hell with it. We'll go back to San Antonio."[17]

Toward the end of 1849, Dutch and his father arrived in the old mission town of San Antonio. In his memoirs, Dutch describes the city as a "long row of adobe, flat-roofed buildings . . . close to the Alamo, [with] grass and pears growing from the roofs. . . . Near the San Fernando Mission, there was nothing but gambling houses and coffee stands; nearly every morning that I had to go to the Market House, I would see from two to three dead men who were killed the night before. I saw Indians camped on the Plazas."[18]

In this wholesome environment, the Wurzbachs made their new home. Jacob, a vigorous man only forty-five years old and an accomplished civil engineer, soon was named superintendent of the San Antonio irrigation system, a job he held for twenty-eight years—until his death in 1879. It was he who undertook the job of restoring the old Spanish irrigation system, which had fallen into ruins after the Spanish mission system collapsed, and returning it to use as a modern irrigation and water supply system.[19]

Probably making the correct assumption that his eleven-year-old Indian-fighter son was not destined to be a scholar, Jacob apprenticed the boy to a local blacksmith. Dutch's later remarks were pithy. "I did not stay long at it, it was too hard work for me. So I went herding mules for the Government on the Salado [Creek]."[20]

Hired by Bvt. Maj. James Belger, assistant quartermaster of the San Antonio Depot, Dutch discovered that herding wild Texas mules was something less than a pleasant bucolic life. He told of a time when the mule wranglers had three hundred of the semibroken creatures inside a corral. Each of the wranglers entered the corral to cut out and rope one of the animals. Little Dutch threw his lariat around a large, bucking animal, who instantly jerked him off his feet and knocked him to the ground. As he struggled there, his lariat wrapped around his leg, and the kicking, bucking, mad-as-hell mule rampaged across the corral, dragging Dutch through the dust, offal, and kicking legs of the other maddened animals. The other wranglers, seeing the boy's plight, charged into the corral, hemmed the raging creature against the fence, and finally freed the battered Dutch.[21]

Shortly after this episode, Dutch was hurt badly when a horse fell on him. Given leave by Major Belger, the injured lad, unable to work, resignedly returned home. When, in 1851, he had recovered, he had a recurrent case of itchy feet. Presumably after his father outlined a choice of either school or a trade, Dutch secretly finagled a job as a teamster and, without informing his father, went west with a wagon train. For the next three years, he worked as a teamster driving mules and oxen, and fighting dust, hail, freezing winds, and scorching sun along the rough roads of the Texas frontier.

The free life of the mule skinner and bull whacker (as those who drove oxen were called) appealed to the gangling teenager. He ranged across frontier Texas, going from Brownsville on the Gulf of Mexico to Franklin (later El Paso) on the western edge of Texas, and from the army supply depot at Corpus Christi on the south coast to Fort Belknap in the heart of Comanche country in North Texas.

Most of the time Dutch freighted for the U.S. Army, supplying the thinly stretched troops of mounted rifles and infantry guarding the pioneer trails west and south of San Antonio. Each of the army freight wagons of those days, pulled by six mules, carried about one and a half tons of supplies. The supply trains, sometimes with a military escort but frequently without one, usually consisted of ten to twenty wagons. The roads of early Texas often were no more than the wagon ruts of preceding trains, and they did not follow the straight and direct routes of modern highways.

On long hauls, the wagons tracked the availability of water and grass. With two men and six mules to a wagon, plus the *remuda* of extra mules, copious amounts of water were required to sustain a train in the hot, dry Texas climate. To keep a mule in good working shape, the animal needed to spend about three hours a day grazing. And in the parched land west of the ninety-eighth parallel, frequent water stops were vital for sustaining life.

Watering, grazing, and driving, if there were no flooded streams, deep arroyos, or plains turned to muddy bogs, a mule train could make fifteen to twenty miles on a good day. During the hot months, the train would travel in early morning and late afternoon. In the hot afternoon hours, it would stop and allow the animals to graze. On the march, the driver handled the reins, while his assistant (called a swamper) rode next to him and handled the brake. Sometimes another teamster rode one of the lead mules.

Freighting across the frontier was a hard and often dangerous job. The traveler alternately froze and boiled in the quixotic Texas weather. However, if he were not crushed as a wagon overturned on the miserably uneven roadways, did not have his brains kicked out by a mule, and did not have his scalp lifted by a Comanche, Apache, Seminole, or Kickapoo, for an adventurous lad there were compensations.

There was the grandeur of an almost virgin land—a mule deer staring with curious eyes from a patch of chaparral, buffalo herds strung out to the horizon, the early morning light on distant mountains under a pale blue sky, and often glorious sunsets. There was rough talk, crude humor, and fierce camaraderie around the campfires; and there was always at least a slight sense of danger, whether from capricious nature or from the roving bands of rapacious Indians. For half-wild lads like Dutch, it must have been a full and exciting life.

The work itself was of vital importance to the settlement and economic development of frontier Texas. Not only did the army posts, supplied by men like Dutch, encourage settlement by putting a damper on Indian raids and thus contribute to agriculture, ranching, mining, and commerce; but also the army's purchase of local goods and services provided a rare cash market for the struggling communities that sprang up around them.

And then there were the fabulous characters whom young Dutch encountered on his far-ranging trips. He recalled: "At one time coming back from El Paso we met Captain Skillman and "Big Foot" Wallace at the painted cave near the crossing of Devil's River; they had just had a fight with Indians and had one man wounded and two mules killed. "Big Foot" Wallace told us they killed some of the Indians, that they must have heard or seen our train coming and left taking their dead with them. We could see blood at different places on the rocks. We stayed with them until evening, they went on and we went to Devil's River to camp."[22]

William A. A. ("Big Foot") Wallace was one of the legendary figures of frontier Texas. A Virginian, he came to the state during the revolt against Mexico, after he learned that his brother and a cousin had been slaughtered at the Goliad massacre. He fought the Mexican army under General Woll in 1842; took part in the ill-fated Mier Expedition, where he drew a white bean; and, after surviving the notorious Mexican Perote Prison, finally was released. Through the War with Mexico, he fought with the famous, or perhaps infamous, Texas Rangers of John Coffee Hays; later, as a Ranger captain, he led his own troop against border bandits and renegade Indians.

When Dutch met him at the Devil's River, he was in his early thirties, standing six feet and two inches without his boots on. His massive shoulders surmounted 240 pounds of bone, sinew, and muscle.

Legendary frontiersman William "Big Foot" Wallace in later years. He and "Dutch" met at the scene of a Comanche raid. Courtesy Institute of Texan Cultures, University of Texas, San Antonio, Texas

His companion—almost forgotten today, but in early Texas, a well-known, even mythical, personage—was Capt. Henry Skillman, also over six feet tall, with a fiery red beard flowing almost to his waist. Often dressed in buckskin, he went about festooned with several revolvers and with Bowie knives hitched about his waist.

Skillman, an easterner by birth, came west as a youth and served as a scout for the Doniphan Expedition during the War with Mexico. When peace came, he settled in Franklin, now El Paso, and in 1851 operated the first mail route from Santa Fe through Franklin, passing from Mescalero Apache country across the Trans-Pecos into Comanche territory on the way to San Antonio. One of his drivers was "Big Foot" Wallace.

While he was a shrewd businessman, Skillman's major passion seems to have been Indian fighting. He often remarked how he "hated Injuns." His battles with the Comanches and Mescaleros made him a legend along the frontier. According to contemporaries, he had one social failing—he would get blind drunk on rot-gut whiskey and ride his snorting and rearing stallion into bars and stores, while firing his pistol into the air.

This little character flaw was to cost Skillman his life. During the Civil War, he sided with the Confederacy. After General Sibley's doomed expedition retreated from New Mexico all the way back to San Antonio, Skillman returned to the El Paso area to operate a spy and guerrilla force which harassed Union troops in the Trans-Pecos area. In April, 1864, he and a few companions, probably sleeping off a drunk, were surprised at their camp near San Elizario, just a few miles downstream from El Paso. Shortly after midnight, Union troops surrounded the camp, which had no guards posted. At the order to surrender, the big redhead groggily chose to shoot it out and so died as he had mostly lived—with a gun in his hand.[23]

These two frontier giants must have been a heady pair of friends for young Dutch, and it is not too much of a guess to believe that he modeled his own early years after the exploits of these two Texas paladins.

On this same trip, sometime between 1851 and 1853, Dutch observed a minor example of frontier justice: "Near Eagle Pass we caught a Mexican trying to steal one of our mules from one of our wagons. We tied him up to one of the wagon wheels and each man taking five licks at him with our whip and then turned him loose."[24]

Of another trip during the same period (Dutch's memoirs are unfortunately imprecise about dates), while transporting army supplies, he wrote: "At one time between Corpus Christi and Fort Ringgold the Indians made a run on us, but we had time to run our train into a fighting corral and whipped them off; we had to drive in a double line for about five miles to camp at a place called Losanos. We had to guard all night as the Indians kept running us all night. In those days when we camped we would run our train into what we called a fighting corral."[25]

Getting the wagons into that defensive formation involved circling the wagons, which was a somewhat complicated maneuver. The train was divided into two sections. When attacked, or in bedding down for the night in dangerous areas, the wagon boss ordered the lead wagon to swing to the left in a big arc designed to bring it back to the road just as the last wagon of the section was leaving it. The second section would perform the same maneuver to the right. The teams would all be swung inward so that their traces could not be cut and they would be protected from arrows or bullets. When the maneuver was completed, the entire train formed a large circle with all the stock inside. Time permitting, spaces between the wagons were crisscrossed with lariats to prevent mounted entry into the train. It was a cumbersome operation, but it made a covered defense possible and undoubtedly saved the scalp of many a mule skinner.

Young Dutch spent three years, from 1851 to 1854, crisscrossing Texas with the military freighters. Relatively speaking, these were calm years on the frontier. But in 1854 the storm broke.

Trouble had been building for a long time. After the annexation of Texas, the federal government assumed "full responsibility for protection against foreign invasion from without and Indians from within."[26] Texas was designated part of the U.S. Eighth Army Corps, with San Antonio as the main depot.

In 1852, the line of frontier forts was extended 150 miles to the west with the establishment of several new forts—Clark, Terrett, McKavett, Johnson, and Phantom Hill. In one of the great incidents of bureaucratic stupidity, the new posts were garrisoned by foot soldiers from the 1st, 5th, and 8th Infantry regiments. If the

Comanches had been an expressively merry race, their laughter might have been heard from the Clear Fork of the Brazos River in the north all the way down to the Rio Grande. And while the number of federal troops in Texas reached a high of 3,265 during 1853, it was ridiculously inadequate for defending the frontier, particularly when most of the soldiers were afoot.[27]

While Dutch was driving mule trains for the army, on January 21, 1853, seventeen-year-old Charles gave up his job on a nearby ranch and traveled to Fort Graham to enlist for five years in the famed Second Dragoon Regiment of the U.S. Army. He was given a routine physical and described as being five feet, four and a quarter inches tall, with gray eyes, brown hair, and a fair complexion. His age, mistakenly or accurately, was given as nineteen. Certifying to his good health was that same Assistant Surgeon Josephus M. Steiner, who less than a year later would kill his commanding officer. During his brief years of schooling, Charles must have received some musical education, for his occupation was listed as musician. He probably started out as a bugler, but he soon was to be promoted.[28]

Meanwhile, the assorted bands of Tonkawa, Kickapoo, Seminole, and Lipan Apaches, as well as the mass of Comanche subtribes, must have spent most of 1853 studying the weaknesses of the Texas defenses. In the spring of 1854, the tribes went on a rampage all along the frontier.

During that fateful season, Dutch was driving mules on a government train that was carrying military supplies from the depot at Corpus Christi on a generally northwestern route to service Fort Merrill, Fort Ewell, and finally Fort Inge, near present-day Uvalde. Fort Inge helped to guard the main road from San Antonio south to Mexico and the western route to California. Dutch's train crossed the Frio River some thirty miles south of the fort and continued on until they approached a ranch owned by Edward Dixon Westfall, located on the banks of the shallow Leona River.[29]

Westfall, a native of Indiana, journeyed to Texas in 1845 and fought in the War with Mexico. Although an educated and well-read man, he "had a natural love for the solitude and romance of the wild woods, and like his erstwhile boon companion Big Foot Wallace, delighted to roam over a new country, shoot game and camp out."[30]

On the banks of the Leona, Westfall was in his element, for Dutch reported that he was the only settler between Fort Inge and Fort Ewell.[31] Romance and solitude, however, claimed a price on the frontier. Like "Big Foot" Wallace and Captain Skillman, Westfall was blue-eyed and unusually tall. Tough and sinewy, he was six feet and four inches in height, and he weighed 190 pounds.

He and Wallace worked as trackers and guides for the army, the Texas Rangers, and the settlers who were filtering slowly into the country. It was said that Westfall knew every mountain, canyon, and cedar break in the area. Indian raiders were well aware of his powers and on many occasions attempted to ambush him during his often lonely travels. During one fight, he killed a Lipan Apache chief called Big Foot, who was seven feet tall and weighed three hundred pounds—perhaps the only man on the frontier who dwarfed "Big Foot" Wallace.

The big fellow was, in fact, the one who gave Wallace his nickname. The scout had had an encounter with the Native American giant some years earlier; and, after he had escaped his wrath, Wallace, looking at the fleeing Indian's tracks, exclaimed, "That buck is wearing moccasins sixteen inches long and five inches wide . . . Boys, I'm going to get that Indian." From then on, William A. became "Big Foot" Wallace.[32]

The night before Dutch's party arrived, however, Westfall was not the hunter but the intended prey of six braves who crept up on him and a black ranch hand when the pair was working a short distance from the ranch house. The attackers, probably Comanches, succeeded in killing the black man, but Westfall made it to his ranch house, where he fought off the war party for more than two hours before they faded away into the chaparral. Dutch helped Westfall bury the unfortunate ranch hand before his train formed up and proceeded to Fort Inge. There they unloaded their much-needed supplies and, after a night's rest, started the long trek back to Corpus Christi. With the Comanches on the warpath, they received an escort of mounted soldiers until they again reached the Westfall ranch.[33]

The next day their escort left the five-team wagon train to its own defenses and returned to Fort Inge, while Dutch and his companions pushed off for Fort Ewell, a pariah encampment about which Lt. Col. Freeman had stated: "A less inviting spot for occupation by troops cannot well be conceived."[34] The fort was situated on the south bank of the Nueces River, at the point where it crossed the San Antonio–Laredo road. Surrounded by salt marsh, the settlement lacked stone and timber for building, had inadequate grazing land, and was subject to flooding for twenty miles around after a heavy rain. The "tumble-down" adobe structures in the camp were roofed mostly with canvas; the troops were riddled with illness.[35]

According to Freeman, if living conditions were lousy, armaments were worse. Some of the mounted riflemen who garrisoned the fort were not issued the Colt revolver, which was the most effective cavalry weapon against mounted raiders. Freeman reported: "The rifle used is an inconvenient weapon for a horseman. It cannot be loaded without dismounting, nor fired with accuracy from the saddle. It is both troublesome and dangerous to carry on horseback without being put in the boot, and when placed there, from its weight, it is almost certain to make the saddle gall the horse's withers."[36]

Officers and men lived in tents without floors, which soon became uninhabitable during the driving rainstorms of late spring and early summer. There was dysentery, diarrhea, fever, and—during most of the year, because "it is impossible to cultivate a garden, on account of the excessive heat, and the want of rain, dew and even moist winds," so that vegetables were lacking—scurvy.[37]

On the night of May 2, Dutch and his companions camped about eight miles from this haven of sick and poorly armed men. The next morning, as the teamsters finished their breakfast and hitched up their teams for the short trip to the fort, Dutch heard shooting to the south, on the far bank of the Nueces River.[38] Urging their teams across the wide and hip-high Nueces, Dutch and his companions arrived at the fort just as a battered survivor stumbled in to pour out a story of ambush and murder.[39]

Charles Russell, one of the surviving teamsters of the ambushed supply train, later recounted what had happened. A train of fourteen wagons, with more than one hundred mules and horses, was traveling from Corpus Christi to Eagle Pass, under the command of Daniel S. McIntosh. The train was within ten miles of the fort when it was attacked.[40]

Shortly before ten o'clock on the morning of May 3, the wagon master, McIntosh, had left the train and ridden off by himself to chase a horse that had gotten loose from the remuda. McIntosh must have been either the most serene and optimistic man on the Texas frontier or, more likely, one of the damnedest fools. Not only did he leave his wagons, but also, trusting in the protection of the scattered military forts or the shield of Divine Providence, he had left Corpus Christi on April 24 with a total armament of only one old rifle for the entire train. On that fateful morning, it happened to be unloaded.

As the wagons lumbered up the side of a hill where the trail was covered on one side by a patch of chaparral filled with scrub oak and mesquite, the teamsters, probably half-groggy from the late morning heat and the sticky humidity occasioned by spring rains, lolled on their wagon seats. "Everything was quiet," Russell wrote, "until the last wagon entered the chaparral." Then the sounds of the sonorous snorting of the mules and the usual cursing of the teamsters were broken by the roar of four rifles fired at close range. Four of the wagon drivers twisted in pain as the slugs ripped through them, while a band of fifteen to twenty Indians burst from the brush.

The attack, Russell recalled, was "so sudden and unexpected that none of us knew there was an Indian near until [they] . . . were in the midst of our train with their lances, charging upon our men from one end [of the train] to the other. The Indians were yelling most horribly."

Their lead mules were grabbed by the attackers, and the unarmed teamsters, unable to turn their wagons across the narrow trail and head for the fort, leaped to the ground and ran for cover in the chaparral. The men wounded in the first fusillade cried for help, but their unarmed comrades had no choice but to abandon them.

As the raiders chased the men through the brush, there began one of the most bizarre battles of the West—the Comanche lance versus the mule skinner's bullwhip. In a newspaper article, Russell described how the hotly pursued teamsters would turn, grab a thrusting lance with one hand, and lash out with their whips against the bare skin of their attackers. Some of the more adroit men, he said, would dive to the ground as a mounted Indian charged, and, before the brave could whirl his horse about, he would dash off into the chaparral.

When thrust by raging braves, the long, feather-bedecked lances, with their razor-sharp points, were vicious and lethal weapons. But perhaps the match was not as uneven as it might at first seem. The braided rawhide whips were twenty feet long, and an expert mule skinner reputedly was able to knock a fly off the ear of a mule twenty feet away without drawing blood. He also, it was said, could "cut the eyes right out of a human opponent's face or slash him to ribbons."[41]

For more than two hours, the teamsters slashed, dodged, and ran through the cactus, cedar brakes, and stump oaks, until all the survivors staggered into the fort. When the first man gave the alarm, a young lieutenant, the only officer present, rose from his sickbed and yelled for a bugler to blast "Boots and Saddles." Spotting Dutch's incoming train, he shouted to its men to saddle their mules and, taking one wagon, join the troops. Within minutes, the relief column was galloping to the scene of the massacre.

Dutch later wrote: "Some eight or ten men had gotten in [to the fort] all scared and bleeding" from wounds inflicted by the Indian lances. "When we got to where the train was I saw a sight I do not wish to see again. The wagons were all scattered along the hillside, some upset, some with front wheels under the beds, some with tongues broken, some standing across the road with broken harness hanging on to them."[42]

McIntosh, the wagon master who had dared Comanche country virtually unarmed, paid a heavy price for his folly. Dutch found his body a hundred yards from the shattered wagons. Strewn around the wreckage were the bodies of two recently discharged soldiers, John McGuire and L. Patterson; Perry Petty of Indiana and a teen-aged boy were found lying near the last wagon.

As Dutch walked to the last body, he was shocked to see the contorted young face of a boyhood friend, August Sartor. Like Dutch, August had journeyed from Germany to Texas with his parents during the 1840s. The Sartor family had made the long trek first to New Braunfels and then to San Antonio, where August's father, a jeweler, had opened a store. Unlike his brother, who also became a jeweler and remained in the city, August became infected with the wanderlust, left school, and sought adventure on the frontier.[43]

The tortured body of his teen-aged friend must have been a horrible sight, even for a sixteen-year-old toughened by life on the Texas frontier. The sight still affected him some sixty years later, as he recounted: "The Indians must have taken four scalps off of his head; there was one cut from ear to ear and another from forehead to back of his neck and four pieces of skin taken off. It was a sorrowful sight."[44]

The soldiers and teamsters loaded the bodies on the wagon and returned them to Fort Ewell, where they were buried. In all, six were killed, two were badly wounded by lance thrusts, and the rest suffered minor wounds. Two poor souls had been taken prisoner, "no doubt to undergo the most horrible tortures." The losses in horses, mules, and cargo were estimated to have amounted to between twenty and thirty thousand dollars.[45]

The following day, Dutch and other members of his train, accompanied by an escort of mounted riflemen, nervously returned to the scene of the massacre to repair and bring back the battered fourteen wagons. While Dutch and four teamsters worked to hitch them up to new teams, the troopers maintained an uneasy guard. Suddenly, from the chaparral came the sounds of hoofbeats and crashing. "Injuns!" someone shouted. The soldier escorts, cursing, spurred their horses and galloped pell-mell back to the fort, as Dutch and his three pals "got between two wagons and fixed to fight." They were braced for battle when their erstwhile attackers burst from the chaparral in the form of several mules who had escaped from the Indians and wandered back to the camp, dragging their harnesses behind them.

As the tension broke, the teamsters were convulsed with laughter, not the usual greeting for the probably still bewildered mules. The returning soldiers, much abashed, were the subjects not only of laughter but also of some uninhibited bawdy revelry by Dutch and his plucky band of mule skinners.

Within a few days, Dutch's train headed southeastward, back to a sobered and frightened Corpus Christi.[46] Interestingly, while raids in that area generally were believed to be the work of Comanches, some of the surviving teamsters, who had lived previously in Florida, said that these attackers were Seminoles, renegades from a band led by a war chief named Wild Cat, who were running loose and raising hell that summer all over Southwest Texas.[47]

The *Colorado Tribune*, a newspaper published in Matagorda and read throughout the Corpus Christi area, did not do much to allay the panic rising with increased Indian violence. The paper wrote of "alarming accounts of continued aggressions of the Indians on the frontier." It followed with an accusation popular among Texans: "So daring have the savages become in their plundering excursions . . . that there remains no longer doubt of a combined invasion by all the tribes . . . instigated and succored by the pusillanimous authorities and people of Mexico." To further frighten its readers, the paper continued, "Inhabitants from advance settlements are flocking . . . into San Antonio for safety."[48]

In the coastal areas of Texas, the prairies were carpeted with belly-high grass and abounded with deer, cattle, wild horses, prairie chickens, and other game birds. Near the clear-running streams, post oaks and brush grew profusely. It was a land not without natural beauty, but the high grass and chaparral-covered watering places unfortunately offered excellent concealment for ambushing Indians.

The Indians in the area were not only bold but also contemptuous. A badly frightened dispatch rider of the Mounted Rifle Regiment staggered into Corpus Christi on May 18 with sore feet and a sorry tale to tell. He had been carrying dispatches from the Corpus Christi Army Depot to Fort Merrill when, as he was approaching the little town of San Patricio, located along the Nueces River some twenty miles northwest of Corpus, a band of Indians "caught him." They grabbed his horse, stripped him, took his mail pouches, and then, with savage contempt, told him that he was free to go. "Return to Corpus Christi and tell your General Persifor Smith what happened to you," they snarled.[49]

Happy to be alive, the messenger made the twenty-mile hike back to the depot with the story of Indian brazenness. The army reacted immediately. A bugler blasted "Boots and Saddles," and a troop of mounted rifles swung into the saddle to track the warriors.[50] A rider was sent on ahead at full gallop to contact the troops at Fort Merrill to join the Corpus detachment. The rider, however, had gotten only five miles from the seaport town when he was spotted racing back to the main body, saying that the Indians had "run him down."

Desperate for reinforcements and unable to reach Fort Merrill, Major Chapman, the depot quartermaster, recruited fourteen teamster volunteers to join the chase.[51] If Dutch was not with them, it probably was the first time he missed a chance to chase Comanches. After viewing with horror what was left of young August Sartor, he might have been one of the more eager volunteers.

To the chagrin of their pursuers, however, the Indians made a clean getaway. They continued raiding in the area, however, and Captain Grainger of the Mounted Rifles wrote to Major Belger at the Corpus Christi Depot, reporting, "Within a week past the Indians have done more mischief than in the last three years. They are chiefly Comanches, with a few Muscolaroes [*sic*] and Lipans."[52]

Stretched thin, the troopers had to patrol in small units, a tactic which easily could lead to disaster if they finally cornered the elusive raiders. Typical was an engagement on May 8, when nine men of the Mounted Rifles ran onto a band of hostile Lipans near Lake Trinidad, forty miles from Corpus Christi. Commanded by Lt.

George B. Crosby, the small patrol attacked more than forty Indians, "routing" them. It was, however, an expensive victory which left the lieutenant "severely wounded in his sword arm" and a sergeant and two troopers killed.[53]

The outlook for getting more troops was poor. On June 19, 1854, Jefferson Davis, secretary of war, wrote to Gen. Persifor Smith, saying that he realized more troops were needed in Texas but that the federal government was unable to furnish reinforcements. Efforts to recruit additional men, he said, were frustrated because of the army's low pay. Suggesting another avenue for gaining reinforcements, Davis authorized General Smith to call upon the governor of Texas for mounted men, who "will be supplied with ammunition, forage, and sustenance by the United States."[54] In other words, it was to be a job for the Texas Rangers.

After a few days in Corpus, Dutch took his teamster earnings, bought several horses, and with two companions headed for San Antonio. Camping for the night at a place he called Rock Springs, Dutch bedded down the horses and then "I went to the spring to get water, the spring was under a bluff, a narrow path leading to it and a live oak tree hanging over it. I laid down to take a drink, and as I started to get up I saw a pair of big eyes looking at me. It was a large leopard cat, ready to jump . . . I did not take time to get up, I pulled my pistol and fired at his neck and jumped. The leopard cat fell in the spring. I had broken his neck . . . I skinned him and brought the skin home with me. It was nine feet long."[55]

A few days later, a tall, strapping sixteen-year-old man, carrying a nine-foot leopard skin, arrived at his father's doorstep in San Antonio. Having vanished more than three years before, the prodigal must have been difficult even for his own father to recognize.

Burned brown by the sun and wind and with muscles hardened, his body was that of a man, not that of the skinny child last seen three years earlier. But the major difference must have been his eyes—crinkled not only by the glare of desert and mountain but also by the grinding hardness of life on the frontier. In his memoirs, he understated as usual: "I took my father by surprise."[56]

CHAPTER 3

The Texas Frontier

In San Antonio there were other surprises. Dutch learned very quickly that his father had remarried and that he had acquired twin sisters.[1]

Whatever welcome he received from his father, Dutch lingered only three weeks in San Antonio. In September, 1854, he signed up as an army teamster to accompany Bvt. Maj. Gen. Persifor F. Smith on a expedition to West Texas to select a site for a new army post designed to guard the trail leading from San Antonio to El Paso del Norte.[2] Fifty-six-year-old General Smith, a hero of the war with Mexico, was one of those few soldiers who, in addition to being an excellent fighter, was also erudite and scholarly and possessed a magnetic personality which inspired both officers and men.

The new outpost was badly needed, for the western trail had received a burst of traffic beginning in 1849, when gold was discovered near Sutter's Mill in California. Soon the trail had become a major thoroughfare for mail carriers, freighters, stage lines, and immigrants.

From the time they left San Antonio, however, travelers were vulnerable to attack by Comanche and Kiowa raiders, who roamed from the plains country of North Texas southward to the interior of Chihuahua, looting and killing anyone insufficiently armed to beat off their sudden forays.

When surviving travelers emerged from the flat plains country of West-Central Texas, they discovered that their trip had taken them only from the griddle into the fire. Entering the eastern edge of the Davis Mountains, they had almost three hundred miles to traverse before reaching the haven of El Paso del Norte and the little town of Franklin. Travelers there were trespassing in the country of the dreaded Mescalero Apaches, who hovered along the trail like birds of prey awaiting a chance to strike. These ferocious raiders would swoop down upon a wagon train or immigrant party, kill all the men, take the women and children as slaves, loot the wagons, and run off or eat the stock. They raided with virtual impunity, because, in early 1854, the 650-mile trip was guarded only by Fort Clark, 130 miles west of San Antonio. The rest of the route, instead of becoming a highway for commerce, was fast turning into an avenue for Apache and Comanche terror.

Setting out in September, General Smith and the regiment of mounted riflemen made the long trek to the settlement of Franklin, on the American side of the Rio Grande across from El Paso del Norte. The burgeoning little border town, later renamed El Paso, was a major stopping place and supply depot for travelers on the way to California. It was the last stop for travelers before setting out across the western desert that extended across southern New Mexico, Arizona, and California. Franklin also was the crossing place for the ancient trail that connected Chihuahua City with the territorial capital of Santa Fe.

After inspecting the American garrison at Fort Bliss, just outside Franklin, General Smith returned to the Davis Mountains. There, on October 5, he bivouacked at a spot called the Painted Comanche Camp, located in a beautiful valley surrounded on three sides by steep cliffs. Earlier, two wagon trains from San Antonio, one of which Dutch had joined, had brought the regiment's headquarters detachment, its band, food supplies, and munitions. Slogging along behind the wagons was the U.S. Army's 8th Infantry Regiment.

How foot soldiers were expected to protect the winding desert and mountain trails against the mounted raiding parties of the Apache and Comanche probably could have been explained by some army bureaucrat in Washington, D.C., but, to westerners, infantry seemed worse than useless. The ineptitude of the poor infantrymen in protecting the route had been detailed earlier by a committee of the U.S. House of Representatives, which had asked, "Can your honorable body conceive of anything more absurd than starting in pursuit of the flying Comanche in a wagon drawn by mules, yet, such your committee are well assured has been done."[3] The *Texas State Gazette*, a newspaper published in Austin, put it more succinctly, stating that foot soldiers were "as useless as lobsters" against mounted Indians.[4]

On October 23, 1854, General Smith named the campsite Fort Davis. It was to guard the Texas-to-California trail for almost four decades, until the last of the Apache renegades, under Geronimo, ended their lives of raiding and surrendered to the U.S. Army in the 1880s.

While the group was returning from Fort Davis, one of many tragic incidents that took place on the frontier ensued. Dutch recounted: "We camped at Ascundos Springs. There was a shot fired and a Mexican belonging to our train was killed. No one saw the shot fired as we were all sitting down eating breakfast."[5]

As the Indian raids increased in ferocity beginning in the spring of 1854, General Smith, realizing that his forces were inadequate to police the frontier, requested Texas governor Elisha Marshall Pease to mobilize six companies of mounted Texas Rangers to campaign alongside his regulars. The governor agreed; however, political considerations delayed the organization of the troops until October.[6]

Dutch, always seeking new adventures, was one of the first to volunteer, enlisting with Capt. Pat Rogers's Ranger company, which was ordered to seek out and fight the dreaded Comanches.[7]

The Comanches were not only the most numerous Indians in Texas but also those most feared. They wandered from what is now Oklahoma as far south as Chihuahua, Mexico, and everywhere they raided relentlessly. A nomadic people, their wealth was in the horses and mules acquired by raiding Mexican and frontier Texas settlements.

The former Republic of Texas President David G. Burnet, who had considerable acquaintance with the tribe, wrote of them: "They have no knowledge of agriculture but depend entirely on game for subsistence, and chiefly on the buffalo, which descend in large herds to their region on the approach of winter. During the summer months when the buffalo return to their northern pastures, these Indians are often exposed to suffering and find it difficult to procure adequate sustenance; but they have a rare capacity for enduring hunger."[8]

"Chiefs are selected," Burnet wrote, "for their prowess in war and for distinction in robbing horses or taking scalps." He pointed out that each band was a law unto itself. "Hence treaties made with these untutored savages are a mere nullity, unless enforced by a sense of fear pervading the whole tribe . . . they have a cherished conceit, the joint product of ignorance and vanity, that they are the most powerful of nations."[9]

"They attack on horseback," Burnet wrote, "sallying out usually by moonlight armed with bow and arrow, lance and any firearms they can obtain, protected by a shield of fire-hardened raw buffalo hide which they believe has magical powers to protect them from enemy bullets."

According to Burnet, those killed outright during a Comanche raid were luckier than the unfortunate white males taken prisoner. The latter were turned over to the women of the tribe, who were said to be "more ferocious and cruel" than the men. Victims were staked out on the ground by day, to be half-cooked by a blazing Texas sun. At nightfall they were dragged to a dance, where they were made to cavort and sing while being beaten with sticks and throngs of rawhide. After a few days, when the Comanches grew bored with a prisoner, they simply killed him. "On some festive occasions they will eat a portion of his flesh," Burnet said.[10]

Robert S. Neighbors, writing to historian H. R. Schoolcraft about the Comanches, pointed out that "the democratic principle is strongly implanted in them." The down side, he said, was that they elected their chiefs on the basis of cunning, knowledge, and success in war.[11] Neighbors wrote, "They are the most expert riders in the world. Men are never taken prisoners by them in battle, but killed and scalped in all cases. The women are sometimes made prisoners, in which case their chastity is uniformly not respected."[12] This was a nineteenth-century euphemism used to suggest that the women were raped.

These people were lords of the plains, the finest light cavalry in the world. From the time when they first secured horses, they had smashed all who had come against them. For more than two hundred years, they foiled the attempts of the Spanish and Mexicans to settle Texas and its hinterlands in safety. It took Manifest Destiny and the Colt six-shooter finally, in the 1870s, to end their dominion over Texas. For it was well-armed Texas settlers, lured by free land and ferociously determined to destroy anyone who threatened their homesteads, who over the years gradually wore the Comanches down.

Historian Rupert Norval Richardson summarized their plight: "Between 1850 and 1860, it may be said that in general the condition of the Comanches was becoming more desperate. They found it more difficult to invade the Mexican frontier, game was becoming scarcer, and, in order to maintain an existence, they had to break up into smaller thieving and marauding bands. . . . But most significant of all, the Texans proved to them that their retreat into the heart of the plains country offered no security."[13]

Perhaps as much sinned against as sinning, the Comanches "found it necessary either to steal or starve."[14] To survive, then, they began intensive raids against the West Texas frontier, from the Clear Fork of the Brazos River to the Rio Grande. It was the need to destroy these ruthless and desperate warriors that led Dutch and his Ranger companions to ride north toward the heart of *Comanchería.*

In the mid-nineteenth century, Texas Rangers were not the professional police investigators they are today. Back then, they perhaps could best be compared to early colonial minutemen. Mostly they were volunteers from local townships who literally took their muskets from fireplace mantles and signed up for ninety days to six months to chase Indians or bandits who were raiding frontier settlements. Professionalism would come much later.

Often they were quite young. Dutch was sixteen years old, unmarried, and unburdened with family responsibilities. Usually Ranger companies did not range too far from their home base, where their members had the love and support of the local citizenry whose sons they were. Because they were trying either to protect or to avenge their homes and families, there was a deadliness of purpose about them.

When, in 1853, a Ranger band rode out of the little settlement of Weatherford to scour the land for Comanche war parties, the women of the town sewed a "costly flag of silk, which had the forcible words: 'NECESSITY KNOWS NO LAW' inscribed across its fold."[15] The message was a lofty way of stating that there would be no judicial proceedings for any captured raiders. No quarter was expected or given.

Before the Weatherford men rode out, they were fired up with an Old Testament scriptural sendoff by the local preacher, a Reverend Byars, who extorted: "Men, as the government has failed to give us protection, the only thing we can do is to march upon these bloodthirsty savages and kill or drive them from the country." At these words, the Rangers cheered and tossed their hats into the air.[16] As the little band rode out, there must have been a scent of sulfur in the air.

Dutch's company of Rangers lingered in San Antonio until fall, when it was put under the command of a Captain Calhoun of the Second Dragoon Regiment. The group's orders were to ride north to Fort Chadborne, an outpost in the midst of Comanche country.[17]

While the Rangers were riding north with the expressed purpose of killing any of the tribesmen they could get into their gun sights, efforts were being made in Austin and Washington, D.C., to achieve a more peaceful solution to the Comanche problem. That intrepid frontiersman, Maj. Robert Simpson Neighbors, one of the few Texans who sympathetically understood the plight of the Indian tribes, long had advocated the establishment of reservations as a solution to frontier defense. In 1853, the Texas legislature agreed and granted twelve leagues of land to the U.S. government for use by Texas Indians. With U.S. Secretary of War Jefferson Davis in agreement, Neighbors and Army Capt. Randolph Barnes Marcy made a reconnaissance into Comanche country. They selected, as a permanent home for the roaming Comanches, an area of more than twenty-three thousand acres on the Clear Fork of the Brazos River, about fifteen miles south of Fort Belknap in modern Throckmorton County.[18]

A smaller reservation of 18,576 acres also was selected about forty-five miles west of Fort Belknap. By September, 1854, two companies of dragoons and two companies of infantry—altogether about 850 men—were sent to reinforce Fort Belknap and to insure the peaceful intentions of the new residents. As it turned out, they also would have to protect the reservation Indians from the Texans.[19]

The reservations were located in traditional Comanche country. Soon more than one thousand Indians, purportedly eager to give up stock stealing and learn the white man's ways of agriculture and stock raising, began to concentrate in the reservation areas. Many Texans, however, remained unconvinced of Comanche sincerity. Indian raids continued all along the frontier, and, although the southern Comanches maintained their innocence, blaming the raiding on their northern brethren and other bands of fragmented tribes roaming West and South Texas, the army and their Texas Ranger allies proceeded with the punitive expedition against the hostiles.

During a trip to the frontier in November, 1854, Neighbors expressed his fear that the campaign would "make no distinction between hostile and friendly Indians" and urged that Gen. Persifor Smith suspend hostilities until all friendly Indians could be settled on reservation lands. Neighbors feared that the punitive expedition might bring on a general Indian war all along the frontier.[20]

In writing to U.S. Commissioner of Indian Affairs George W. Manypenney, Neighbors pointed out: "It is certainly strange that one department of the government should employ agents to make peace, select lands for permanent settlements, and induce large bodies of Indians to hold themselves in readiness for settling down, and another should assemble troops in the same neighborhood to make war on the same Indians."[21] Perhaps he was naïve in assuming that one branch of the federal government knew, or could influence, what another branch was doing.

As Neighbors continued his struggle to make peace, Dutch and the Rangers were accumulating supplies. Mustered into federal service in November, they departed from San Antonio in December, 1854, for the 180-mile ride to Fort Chadborne, where they would rendezvous with two more companies of Rangers and the Second Dragoons.[22]

After reaching Fort Mason, about halfway to their destination, the small garrison there reported hostiles raiding in the area. A squad of ten Rangers, including Dutch, was placed under the command of young 2d Lt. John Rogers and was detailed as forward scouts to trail the hostiles.[23]

Scouting along the trail, Rogers, Dutch, and their eight companions found signs of Indians near the San Saba River. Urging on their tired horses, the troop caught up with the Indians near the head of Brady Creek. The raiders were camped on a hilltop, eating a meal, their horses grazing. The little band of scouts began creeping up to the unsuspecting camp until, when they were within half a mile and just about ready to charge, they were spotted.

Abandoning packs and loot, the startled war party leaped upon their horses' backs and, whipping them unmercifully, fled at a wild gallop. Dutch and his companions took up the chase with shouts. Across the freezing prairie they rode, horses lathering even in the cold wind, while the cursing Rangers spurred their mounts in a wild frenzy. The Rangers kept up the chase for twelve miles, until their lightly equipped quarry was able to outdistance and lose the pursuers. Carrying only a few supplies, the Rangers returned to the Indian camp to retrieve two stolen mules and the abandoned loot.[24]

In the meantime, the main column had continued its march. Dutch and the scouts, with dwindling supplies, were left to trek more than 120 miles to Fort Chadborne. They marched across rolling prairie, populated for the most part by prairie-dog towns, some "covering an area of a mile square."[25] When their supplies ran out, Dutch remembered, "we lived on deer and prairie dog meat for four days."[26]

Fort Chadborne was established in October, 1852, by two companies of the U.S. 8th Infantry Regiment, on a site about halfway between the modern towns of Abilene and San Angelo. A short distance from Oak Creek, a small tributary of the Colorado River, the location ominously was called Tan-tan-se, o-ah-keep-Hoo-nough, or, in English, Mosquito Creek. Sadly, the Indian name was the more accurate description.

The post was a conglomeration of stone-walled buildings with shingled roofs and huts made of scrub oak and mesquite logs, located in the very heart of the territory occupied by Chief Buffalo Hump's Peneteka Comanches. While water was in short supply, grazing was "excellent." That and the regimental band, "the finest in Texas," according to Colonel Freeman, were Fort Chadborne's only redeeming assets.[27]

There was not much in the way of entertainment except for an occasional horse race. On one occasion, a Comanche chief named Mu-la-que-top brought to the post "a miserable sheep of a pony, with legs like churns; a three-inch coat of rough hair stuck out all over the body; and a general expression of neglect, helplessness, and patient suffering." Challenged by some of the post officers to race this pride of Comanche horseflesh against one of their own blooded steeds, the chief reluctantly agreed. The Comanches bet their prized buffalo robes and other items of plunder against the officers money, flour, and sugar that their nag could beat a fine Kentucky mare, reputedly the third fastest horse on the post.

A distance of four hundred yards was paced off, and a lithe young cavalryman climbed into the saddle of one of Kentucky's finest. A big, lumbering, 170-pound Comanche carrying a big club mounted the raggedy Indian horse. When the starting flag was dropped, the Comanche jockey hit his poor beast a whale of a thump on the rump and let out a bloodcurdling yell. The horse practically flew along the improvised race track and galloped to the finish line, beating the Kentuckian by a neck.

The Comanches cheered wildly and did impromptu war dances; the officers cursed and grumbled. Considering the race a fluke, the officers challenged the Comanches to another race, at double the stakes. Bringing out their second fastest horse, in less than an hour they were ready for the second race. It was run, and Mu-la-que-top's raunchy-looking nag won again. More war dances and more grumbling.

As Col. Richard Irving Dodge reported it, "The officers, thoroughly disgusted, proposed a third race, and brought to the ground a magnificent Kentucky mare, of the true Lexington blood, and known to beat the best of the others at least forty yards in four hundred." The Comanches, crazed with excitement, heaped up their winnings and all their other goods, as the officers bet just about everything but their weapons. Gloating, the gentlemen of the post figured they had suckered the dancing and shouting Indians into a financial disaster.

At the start, the big Comanche jockey threw away his club and gave a piercing war cry. The Indian horse "pricked up his ears" and bounded away like the wind. The Comanche was so far ahead that he twisted around and rode the last fifty yards face to tail, "making hideous grimaces and beckoning to the rider of the mare to come on."[28]

The officers got revenge later, when the post doctor got in a supply of either ether or chloroform. The physician boasted to a group of Comanches huddled in his hospital tent that his medicine was so powerful that he could kill a man with the wave of a handkerchief and then, within a few minutes, bring him back to life. He asked for a Comanche volunteer to undergo this remarkable metamorphosis, but not a warrior came forward.

As a substitute for the reluctant braves, a Comanche dog was brought in, and all agreed that the poor mutt was the proper vehicle for demonstrating the white man's magic. As the cringing animal was placed in front of the doctor, the latter unobtrusively poured some of the anesthetic over a rag and then, with a waving of arms and a babble of abracadabra, passed the rag over the dog's nose.

The animal stiffened and then went inert, as the Indians gasped. The doctor declared, "The dog is dead." To prove it, he grasped a small hatchet and, with a mighty blow, cut off a section of the animal's tail. The dog neither moved nor let out a whimper. "Surely the dog is dead," the Comanches agreed. The animal lay "dead" for several minutes. Then the doctor began to chant incantations in an unknown tongue. Slowly the animal began to stir. As it awoke, it suffered a sudden spasm of pain from the region of its amputated tail. Letting out a terrified howl, the dog got to its feet and, tucking what was left of its missing appendage between its legs, raced squealing out of the tent. The Indians, eyes widened in terror, raced pell-mell after the fleeing dog.[29]

Among junior officers stationed at Fort Chadborne during the 1850s were Lt. James Longstreet and Lt. George E. Pickett, who a decade later were to play decisive roles more than one thousand miles to the east, at a little Pennsylvania country town named Gettysburg.

But life at the fort was not all horse races and jokes. While the Comanches could be friendly one day, they could be devils incarnate the next. Earlier in 1854, they had killed a Captain Van Buren only a few miles from the post and a few weeks later had intercepted two soldiers serving as mail couriers, tied them to a tree, and burned them to death. Later, passengers on the Butterfield stagecoach line saw Comanches rustle a small herd of horses right under the noses of a mounted patrol, only a few miles from the fort. On another occasion, a soldier ambushed near the post staggered into the parade ground with fourteen arrows protruding from his body. Surprisingly, the human porcupine was treated successfully by the post doctor and survived.[30]

When Dutch's tired and hungry little scouting party finally rode into Fort Chadborne, the post was bustling with activity. Two other companies of Texas Rangers (officially, they were called Texas Mounted Volunteers) and two troops of the Second Dragoons beefed up the garrison for the coming campaign.

After Dutch's troop was fed and quartered, he took a stroll across the parade ground. As he was walking, he saw what he thought was a familiar-looking youth wearing a natty Dragoon uniform with three big stripes on the sleeve. Getting closer, he yelled, "Charlie, Charlie," and broke into a run. The erect youth turned, looked startled for a second, and then, with a joyous yelp, hollered "Dutch, Dutch," and he too broke into a run. After a four-year separation with no communication, the two brothers embraced and happily pounded backs in the middle of the parade ground.[31]

After a few days, the brothers, each with his respective command, marched sixty miles to the northeast, over a rough and poorly marked trail, to fabled Fort Phantom Hill, where they awaited further orders. The most poignant remark ever uttered about that awful place was made by Colonel Freeman, who pointed out in his report that water had to be hauled from a creek four miles away and that the nearest source of fuel was a thicket eight miles from the fort. Freeman wrote, "It would really be a charity to remove the garrison."[32]

The U.S. 5th Infantry Regiment had founded the post in 1851 to protect California-bound travelers, who were frequently the prey of Comanche raiders. The post seemed cursed from the start. Maj. J. J. Abercrombie, the founding officer, reported that a November "norther" froze to death one teamster, twenty horses, and numerous mules and oxen.

While travelers were protected as well as foot-slogging infantry could protect a moving wagon train, the garrison itself was in feverish need of protection from the brackish, silty, and unsanitary river water, the only water available. After many of the garrison fell ill, a scout found the source of infection—decaying buffalo carcasses in the river bed. Later, four miles from the post, a well was dug, which provided reasonably good water. For lack of fresh vegetables, however, the post suffered from scurvy. There also was intermittent fever, dysentery, and pneumonia.

One of the loneliest posts on the frontier, Phantom Hill offered only long hours of patrol, burning heat, freezing cold, and the opportunity to die miserably from a Comanche arrow or lance thrust. Phantom Hill was abandoned in disgust in April, 1854. Probably to make sure they never had to return to the place, some enlisted men burned it to the ground.

When the Rangers and the Dragoons entered the fort during the winter of 1854–55, it was being used as a temporary base; only skeletal remains of the buildings and their fire-blackened chimneys stood, like eerie sentinels in the twilight of the rolling prairie country. Even the name *Phantom Hill* was a testament to the general unpleasantness of the place. The name originated, it was said, when a nervous sentry fired his rifle one night at an imaginary foe. His sergeant cursed him for firing at phantoms, and the name stuck.[33]

After waiting a week, the assembled troops got orders to move a hundred miles to the north, to the Little Wichita River, in present Archer County. There, rumor had it, all of the northern Comanche tribes had assembled to vie with the American forces for the high plains.

As the main body moved out, Dutch again went ahead with a small twelve-man scouting party to search for signs of Indians. The scouts spotted Comanche tracks soon after leaving the fort and for two days and nights followed the trail across the plains. On the third day, while the scouts stopped in a little grove to rest, Dutch had "the worst scare I ever got." Half-dozing, half-alert for a surprise attack, he heard a noise behind him, whirled around, grabbed his rifle, and yelled, "*Indians!*"

Sleeping men fought out of their stupor, seized weapons, and prepared to sell their lives dearly. But Dutch muttered a few words not heard in polite circles of that day. There was nothing "but a big opossum close to where I lay." Amid a few ribald comments about what Dutch and the opossum could do to each other, the men returned to a fretful sleep.

The Indian signs played out, so Dutch and the others rejoined the main body and remained with them until the expedition arrived at the Little Wichita, only to find that the Comanches had been alerted and had fled.

Leaving their supply wagons with a small guard at the Little Wichita base, the expedition made a forced march north to the Red River in pursuit of their elusive foe, but finally they lost the trail. Returning to the Little Wichita camp, they planned to rest their exhausted horses for a few days. Upon their arrival, however, they spotted an ominous bluish haze to the north, coming toward them at high speed.

A few hours later, howling winds and driving snow hit the camp. With the horses too drained to travel, the troops dug in and huddled and shivered together for two weeks until the weather broke and they were able to make a short march to Fort Belknap, overlooking the Salt Fork of the Brazos River.

The blizzard that nearly froze Dutch and his companions was the same one described so vividly by Eliza Johnston, wife of Col. Albert Sidney Johnston. She was traveling with her husband, who was leading the newly formed 2nd Cavalry Regiment on a march from Jefferson Barracks near St. Louis to Fort Belknap.

Colonel Johnston, later one of the major military figures of the Confederacy, died of wounds sustained while commanding a Rebel army during the Battle of Shiloh in April, 1862. On the march to Fort Belknap, his regiment contained many of the men who would command the southern armies during the Civil War. A few of his officers were Lt. Col. Robert E. Lee, Capt. E. Kirby Smith, Lt. John Bell Hood, and Lt. J. E. B. Stuart.

As the regiment traveled through North Texas during the Christmas season, Eliza recorded:

> Dec. 22: . . . at eight o'clock the coldest norther I ever felt . . . impossible to keep warm . . . 4 degrees below zero.

> Dec. 23: Could not march, the wind blowing almost a hurricane . . . cold bitter cold.

> Christmas Day: Shivering around a camp fire to keep life in us . . . so cold we could not march . . . about 35 miles to Fort Belknap.
>
> Dec. 26: . . . 2 degrees below zero.
>
> Dec. 29: One degree below zero and sleeting.[34]

Finally the regiment camped a mile from the fort and, when the weather abated, continued its march south. A winter campaign on the plains of North Texas was not for the fainthearted.

Dutch's Ranger company was mustered out of service in March, 1855. While its members did not fight the big battle against the Northern Comanches that they had hoped for, the expedition had not been a total failure. By driving the Northern Comanches north of the Texas border at the Red River, the troops had protected the harried frontier settlements from the burden of Comanche raids—at least for a short while.

If the Rangers and Dragoons had been partially successful, Neighbors's attempts to settle the Southern Comanches on two Texas reservations had met with total frustration. By early spring, Buffalo Hump and almost eight hundred Comanches had settled on the Clear Fork Reservation. Shortly after their arrival, however, a Comanchero named Leyndecker, who sold guns and whiskey to the Indians, told Buffalo Hump that the large number of troops at Fort Chadborne was planning to attack him. Always suspicious, Buffalo Hump and his Penateka tribesmen fled westward from the Clear Fork, and Neighbors's hard work was all for naught.[35]

After his discharge, Dutch, with his San Antonio *compadres*, made a 250-mile ride south to San Antonio, arriving "about the last of April." He stayed a few weeks visiting his father and then was off on another adventure.[36]

CHAPTER 4

Mexican Adventure

In the early summer of 1855, Dutch signed on as a teamster to accompany a detail of the Second Dragoons being deployed from Texas to Fort Riley, Kansas, as that state became embroiled in a bloody struggle over the issue of slavery. The Kansas struggle was a precursor to the bloody fratricidal war, half a decade later, between North and South.

The troops began their trek from Fort Belknap across the boiling hot Staked Plains of North Texas and through the Indian Territory (now Oklahoma), arriving at Fort Riley in September. During the trip, Dutch later recalled, "There was no house nor white man to be seen, on the trip all I saw was Indians and buffaloes. The Dragoons had a good time killing buffaloes."[1]

Dutch stayed in Kansas until spring of 1856, making freight runs between Fort Riley and Fort Leavenworth. "It was the coldest country I ever saw, for we had to drive in snow and ice all the winter."[2] He started for home in April, 1856.

Journeying to St. Louis, Dutch "got on the first steamboat I ever saw."[3] He traveled by paddle-wheel steamboat from St. Louis to

New Orleans during the heyday of river transportation, upon waters made famous by Samuel Clemens (Mark Twain). As an apprentice pilot, Clemens plied the profitable but treacherous route along the Mississippi River. After arriving at the sultry and—as it must have struck him—most exotic port of New Orleans, Dutch took a coastal steamer to Indian Point, Texas. He made the final lap to San Antonio on a newly established stage line. After a short visit with his family, he again succumbed to wanderlust.

Troops were on the move, and Dutch joined a supply train accompanying detachments of the Mounted Rifle Regiment, bound for New Mexico, and elements of the First Dragoon Regiment, heading for Arizona and California. Following the now established trail, the large convoy traveled from San Antonio to the Mexican border at Eagle Pass, then crossed increasingly arid terrain to Fort Lancaster, Fort Davis, and El Paso. From there the party trekked across the desert to Fort Fillmore and Fort Thorn, in the comparatively lush Mesilla Valley of New Mexico. Then it crossed rugged desert and mountain country en route to Tucson.

The troops were welcomed with wild enthusiasm by the handful of American citizens at Tucson, as well as by the resident Mexican population. Even after the Gadsden Purchase of 1853, which turned the area over to the Americans, Mexican troops had stayed on until, over the protests of all the inhabitants, they finally withdrew to Mexico in March, 1856. The withdrawal left the settlers at the mercy of the Chiricahua, White Mountain, Pinal, and Coyotero Apache bands, who proceeded to raid with impunity throughout Arizona and the Mexican state of Sonora. When Dutch and the convoy of supply wagons and troops arrived in Tucson in November, 1856, they were a most welcome sight.

After resting a few days, three companies of Dragoons, under the command of Maj. Enoch Steen, left the column to journey about forty miles south to establish Fort Buchanan, close to the border between Arizona and Sonora. The rest of the column marched west, seventy miles across the desert, from Tucson to Maricopa Wells.

The route trailed north along the Santa Cruz River until it joined the Gila River at Maricopa Wells. The trail was pioneered by Lt. Col. Philip St. George Cooke, who, in December, 1846, during the War with Mexico, led his small army of some three hundred Mormon volunteers along it on the way to southern California. Their passageway later was called the Southern Overland Route, and soon, after gold was found near Sutter's Mill in 1849, large numbers of gold-crazed would-be prospectors followed its dusty trail to California.

Reaching the wells, the troops spent two weeks "to let the teams rest" and to take on a large supply of water before tackling the dry, barren forty-five-mile stretch of desert between the wells and the bend of the Gila River, where it swings south to flow eventually into the Colorado River near Yuma.[4]

After the teams were rested, Dutch, with the supply train and eight companies of the First Dragoons, traveled "forty-five miles without water to the Gila River." He later recalled: "We had to travel down the Gila River to Fort Yuma without feed for our teams . . . all we could get for our mules was cottonwood brush; we left a good many of our mules and horses and wagons on the road. We passed where the Oatman family were massacred some time before we passed. We saw the graves and old pieces of wagons laying about."[5]

Less than two years earlier, on April 18, 1854, in one of Arizona's grisliest massacres, a Tonto Apache band of nineteen warriors had attacked the Oatman family while the latter was preparing to cross the Gila River. The father, mother, and one son were butchered; another son, Lorenzo, was clubbed and left for dead; while two daughters, Olive, twelve years old, and Mary Ann, eight, were kidnapped. Lorenzo was found and nursed to health by friendly Pima Indians. Mary Ann died in captivity; it was five years before Olive was ransomed and set free by a detachment of U.S. cavalry.

By the time Dutch's caravan crossed the desert to reach the Yuma Crossing on the Colorado River, most of the Dragoons' horses had died from thirst or exhaustion, and the men were afoot.[6]

The crossing itself was notorious for scenes of robbery and murder. In 1849, a ferry had been built by an army lieutenant to transport a military survey party. Later, a Dr. Abel Lincoln took over the ferry; charging one dollar per person and two dollars per horse, ox, or mule, he quickly made more than sixty thousand dollars from travelers lured to the California goldfields. This lucrative trade proved to be a beacon that drew a notorious scalp-hunter and all-around thug named John Joel Glanton to move in on Lincoln and kill off the Yuma Indians who operated a competing ferry. Glanton and his gang enjoyed a monopoly on the ferry business until he, Lincoln, and his band of cutthroats in turn were ambushed and killed by an avenging band of Yumas in April, 1850. In one of the tales of lost treasure so common throughout the West, Glanton is reputed to have buried fifteen thousand dollars in gold near the crossing. For the past century and a half, star-crossed prospectors have been digging up the desert sands to find Glanton's gold. Needless to say, it never has been found.

It was not gold, but rather the hope of fresh water, decent food, a much-needed bath, and a rest from the trail that encouraged the ragged band of Dragoons and teamsters who finally staggered into Fort Yuma. The place offered a welcome rest after their journey of more than a thousand miles across the southwestern desert.

After the teamsters had unloaded their cargo, collected their pay, and rested up in the little desert town for two weeks, events occurred that once again whetted Dutch's ongoing appetite for action and adventure. Around that time, a hard-looking man named Clint Thompson sauntered into the camp and gave Dutch and his friends a recruiting spiel about filibustering into Mexican Sonora with Gen. Henry A. Crabb.[7]

The twisted and bloody tale of Crabb's 1857 expedition from California into Sonora, Mexico, is laced with contradictions and recriminations and salted with border hatreds and fears. The events which overtook the little army, led by Crabb to tragic destruction, can be traced only through the fragmentary correspondence which survives and the perhaps prejudiced reports of the few survivors.

Crabb, a Tennesseean and an ardent southerner, had ventured

out to California before the Gold Rush days of 1849. There he married Philomena Aiensa, whose parents reportedly had been driven from their vast landholdings in Sonora because of their loyalty to the Spanish crown. Active in California state politics, Crabb became associated with William Walker, a fellow Tennesseean and a frail dreamer whose visions of carving out a new empire in Latin America ultimately led him, in 1859, to face a Nicaraguan firing squad.

Both were members of the Knights of the Golden Circle, a secret organization of southerners who planned to create a slave kingdom that would be greater than the Roman Empire. The name came from a proposal that envisioned Havana, Cuba, as the center of a circular empire with a radius of twelve hundred miles and encompassing the border states of Maryland, Kentucky, and southern Missouri; all of the American southern states; parts of Kansas, Texas, and Mexico; all of Central America; the West Indies; and the northern part of South America. This fantasy empire would corner most of the world's production of tobacco, cotton, sugar, rice, and coffee. It would stretch around the Gulf of Mexico like a giant circle of gold.

Crabb was to seize his portion of the empire in the state of Sonora, Mexico. In the 1850s, the political confusion in that province embodied in microcosm that of the larger Mexico itself, which had lost half its territory to the *gringo* invaders in 1848. The fury of contesting Mexican political factions was fueled by pain at the humiliation of their country and the grim toll taken on their smashed armies. Throughout northern Mexico, despair turned into desperation as marauding Apache bands scourged isolated haciendas. These fierce raiders left *rancheros* stripped of livestock, men butchered, women raped, and children carried off into captivity. In Sonora the chaos was, if possible, even worse, as the Yaqui Indians, perennial foes of Spanish *conquistador* and Mexican alike, turned the fury of their xenophobia against all comers.

To the hordes of buccaneers, assorted cutthroats, and hard cases who had congregated along the Barbary Coast near San Francisco, Sonora seemed ripe to be plucked from the already battered Republic of Mexico. In the early 1850s, the French soldier of fortune Comte Gaston Raousset de Boulbon and a band of renegades captured the coastal city of Guaymas and drove inland as far as Hermosilla before being wiped out by an aroused Mexican people. In 1854, William Walker (possibly accompanied by Crabb) launched a buccaneering expedition into Baja California and declared an independent republic incorporating the states of Baja and Sonora. Again a weary people rose to repel the invaders from the North.

Little dismayed by the failures of these previous expeditions, Crabb in 1856 tried a more subtle approach. When his political ambitions were frustrated in California because of his fanatical southern partisanship, he turned to Sonora. Crabb visited the Mexican state, accompanied by his wife and his brother-in-law, Jesus Aiensa. While there, he made contact with the deposed governor, Ignacio Pesqueira, who at the time was jockeying for power with his archenemy Manuel María Gándara, then Sonora's governor. The two leaders typically fluctuated among lead bullets, crooked ballots, flagrant bribery, and unfaltering chicanery in their efforts to seize power. At this particular time, Pesqueira was out and Gándara was in.

Undoubtedly some agreement was reached between Crabb and Pesqueira, although Pesqueira for the rest of his life denied it. Crabb and his partisans, however, maintained that the agreement went something like this: Crabb would supply Pesqueira with arms and money, as well as recruit fighting men to put him back in power. Crabb, in addition, would defend the northern boundaries of the state by ruthlessly suppressing the marauding Apaches. In payment for these services, large tracts of land in northern Sonora, as well as mineral rights to the gold and silver mining areas in the fertile Assumption Valley near the Gulf of California, would be awarded to Crabb and his band of condottieri. A cynic, or simply a student of the period, might suspect that each side had planned a double cross.

Upon his return to San Francisco, Crabb began to recruit his army of "peaceful immigrants." Much of the financing, as well as many of the leaders of the expedition, reportedly came from the clandestine Knights of the Golden Circle. The group's original goal had been to make California a slave state allied with the Deep South. But Union sentiment was running strong in 1856, and many of these men who were holding political office in California were defeated in the state elections that year. A motley group of recruits was gathered from the ranks of these frustrated politicians, as well as from groups of disappointed gold seekers, freelance gunmen, and young adventurers like Dutch.

In December, 1856, Crabb and his advance party set sail from San Francisco and came ashore at a point near Los Angeles. There they bought wagons and pack animals for the long trek across the California and Arizona deserts. Crabb, with an advance guard of about a hundred men, proceeded overland to the district capital of Altar in Sonora. His plan was to rendezvous there with the main body of a thousand men under "General" John D. Cosby, who would sail from San Francisco to Port Lobos on the Mexican coast, then march fifty miles to the rendezvous. Pesqueira, with the support of the populace, would join them, and the grand settlement scheme would begin.

Cosby, left behind in San Francisco to recruit and equip the main army, unfortunately was displaying signs of newly acquired affluence. Sporting a brand new carriage and a twin span of fine thoroughbred horses, he whooped it up in Frisco's bars and bordellos. Unbeknownst to Crabb, he never recruited another force.

Unaware that his main army did not exist, Crabb, thin-lipped, lean-shanked, with piercing blue eyes and a stiff spade beard, sat astride his mount, inspected his men, surveyed the expanses of rugged desert terrain, and gave the command to march. They moved southeastward along the Colorado River to a point near Yuma, then headed east toward the Gila River to an appropriately named Filibusteros Camp. For both men and animals, struggling through the sand hills of the California-Arizona desert was a special brand of hell. Their wagons, most of their pack animals, and many of the men broke down under the strain of the desert's searing heat.

While resting at Filibusteros Camp on the Gila River in Arizona, the men delighted in carving their names on the surrounding scrub oaks. It was to be their most lasting memorial. With the surviving pack animals and one remaining wagon, they pushed off, marching southeast along the barren Lechugilla Valley until they reached water at the Tinajas Altar, or high tanks—potholes excavated in the granite mountains by storm waters. In these rancid potholes they found just enough potable water to enable them to survive. Continuing on, by early March they reached the barren trading post at Sonoita, just north of the Arizona-Mexico boundary. There they set up a permanent camp.

To encourage his bone-weary men, Crabb announced that each man would be deeded 160 acres of land once Sonora was secured. Henceforth, he told them, he would be called "governor" rather than "general." In an effort to increase his striking force, he sent agents to Tucson and to a camp of Texas miners prospecting near Tubac.

One of Pesqueira's cronies, however, brought ominous news from the interior. Pesqueira, he said, had ousted Governor Gándara and seized power in Sonora. Crabb was no longer needed. Pesqueira reasoned, moreover, that, if the authorities in Mexico City learned of his negotiations with Crabb, it was very likely to be an adobe wall, a last cigarette, and a final look down twelve rifle barrels for the newly installed governor.

"Go back or be killed" was the essence of his terse communiqué to Crabb, but the latter was not to be turned back so easily. In a letter to Mexican officials, he accused Don José María Redondo, prefect of the district of Altar, of poisoning wells along his route of march and inciting the Papago Indians against him. Maintaining that his band was bent on "peaceful settlement" under the colonizing laws of Mexico, he warned: "If blood be shed, it will be upon your head." He would march on, he announced.

On March 26, Crabb and seventy men began the 120-mile trek across the appropriately named Camino del Diablo (Devil's Highway). Twenty men under Capt. Freeman McKinney, with new recruits from the Knights of the Golden Circle, followed more slowly.

Footsore animals and men too sick to climb into a saddle were left behind, under the command of Crabb's brother-in-law, Jesus Aiensa.

If the march from Los Angeles to Sonoita had been hell, it was a minor hell compared to the one the band confronted now. For the Camino del Diablo was a barren wasteland. Flanked by granite mountains, the men marched through barren sandy valleys criss-crossed by dry arroyos. Along the faint trail, they avoided the sharp-spined giant *saguaro* cacti, which cast demonic shadows across the trail, and the sprawling *ocotillo* (called "The Devil's Coachwhip"), which, when brushed, could rip a shirt and tear an arm with evil ease. Only a smattering of *palo verde*, clustered protectively in dry washes, occasionally offering some slight shelter against the moaning, sandy winds that swept the route. Again the horses and mules began to falter and then die from exhaustion and lack of water.

Scouts and spies began to bring back the ominous word that Pesqueira was rousing the country against the *norteños*. In a call to arms, one Pesqueira message exhorted his countrymen, "Show no mercy . . . let them die like wild beasts . . . liberty or death . . . Viva México . . . death to the filibusters."

It was on April Fool's Day, 1857, that Crabb's men reached the outskirts of Caborca. The town's *jefe* and chief of militia, Capt. Lorenzo Rodríquez, rode out to negotiate with the Americans. Accounts varied as to how the fighting began. The Americans claimed that they were ambushed and fired upon without warning. The Mexicans asserted that Rodríquez was shot down in cold blood as he rode up to the *gringo* invaders. The first shot, whoever fired it, was followed by volleys of gunfire from both sides. After a charge by Mexican cavalrymen was beaten back, riflemen from the village slipped behind adobe fences on both sides of the road and opened fire. But the disciplined fire of Crabb's men became too intense. Leaving ten to fifteen dead, the Mexican forces retreated to the town, where most of the women and children of the village fled to the old mission church, La Iglesia Caborca. Their men fought house to house through the dusty unpaved streets, as the whooping Americans attacked continually and fearlessly.

After an afternoon of fierce fighting, the outgunned Mexican militia retired to the old mission. As their women lighted candles and prayed at the altar, the Mexicans lined the church roof and windows, keeping up a constant harassing fire against the invading forces.

Crabb's men occupied a row of three adobe buildings facing the church. Using rifle butts, they knocked loopholes out of the dried mud walls and opened a hot fire upon the Mexican defenders. Expert riflemen for the most part, and shooting at a range of less than one hundred feet, they took a deadly toll on the defenders. As darkness fell, the shooting died out except for the occasional crack of a sharpshooter, and the exhausted men of both sides fell into an uneasy sleep.

Unbeknownst to Crabb, the nearby hills were beginning to swarm with fifteen hundred armed men under the command of Col. Hilario Gabilondo. The small band of Americans, running low on ammunition and water, kept up the siege throughout April 2 and 3. The battle was hot, bloody, and inconclusive. On the night of April 3, Crabb launched a bold attempt to take the beleaguered mission turned fortress. With a dozen volunteers, Crabb, cradling a keg of gunpowder, dashed across the courtyard and fought his way into the convent rooms by the side of the church. After a bitter hand-to-hand struggle, in which Bowie knife and rifle butt vied in rending flesh and cracking bones, the convent rooms were secured.

Placing the powder keg against the heavy wooden door of the church, Crabb lit a short fuse and ducked. But the fuse had become dampened and sputtered out. Crabb, shot in the right arm, yelled to his men to retreat. Leaving three dead, his battered band recrossed the square to the safety of the loopholed adobe walls, where they sank to the earthen floor exhausted.

By the next morning, April 4, failure had turned to disaster. Gabilondo, with reinforcements including cavalry units from Santa Cruz, Tubac, and the former garrison of Tucson, along with the Tuape volunteer infantry, had arrived and surrounded the Americans' position. The besiegers had become the besieged.

On April 5, more infantry reinforcements came up and wheeled into position. For two days they kept up a series of attacks, as Crabb's men exhausted food, water, and most of their ammunition. Then Gabilondo was reinforced by a band of Pahpah Indians armed with bows and arrows. Squatting in the church grounds, they began tying old rags and straw refuse to their arrows. On April 6, two cannon, trundled from El Altar by oxcart, arrived. Gabilondo was ready for the final assault.

A large Mexican flag was broken out from the belfry of the old church. The cannon were wheeled into position and began opening fire on the three adobe houses held by the buccaneers. Soon the supply of cannonballs was exhausted, and the artillerists began firing scrap iron, stones, and anything that looked lethal. Shouting "¡Viva México!" and "¡Mueran los gringos!" ("Death to the gringos!"), the Mexican troops launched furious assaults all day.

At nine o'clock that night, the Pahpah Indians were ready. Fitting the arrows wrapped in cloth and straw to their bowstrings, they set them alight and fired. The arrows arched over the square and buried themselves in the thatched and wooden roofs beneath which Crabb's men were holding out. After repeated volleys, the roofs were set ablaze; soon the houses were filled with leaping flames and acrid, billowing smoke.

Losing the battle against the enveloping flames, Crabb, in a last-ditch effort, brought up two of his remaining barrels of gunpowder and heaved them up onto the burning roofs, in an effort to blast the blazing beams away. With a mighty roar, the gunpowder exploded, partly extinguishing the flames. But it was a costly victory, for Crabb and his men were scorched and half-smothered by blast and smoke.

Then Gabilondo made an offer. Surrender, the men were told, and they would be treated as prisoners of war. A doctor would be provided to treat their wounds. Even better, the officer promised, they would be given free, unimpeded passage to the border.[8]

While Crabb was pondering this offer, Dutch, with four of his friends as well as other strays who had volunteered for Crabb's army, were riding hard to reinforce him. Whether Clint Thompson had offered them land, gold, or glory is not known; but Dutch, with his characteristic yen for adventure, likely joined up just for the hell of it.

Thompson had provided horses and supplies to the volunteers. The night before they departed Fort Yuma, a sergeant of Dragoons sold them four carbines, four "Army pistols," and two hundred cartridges for two hundred dollars. The next day, the band, with its undoubtedly stolen weapons, rode east. After traveling a few miles, the group was overtaken by the sergeant, disguised in civilian clothes, who, adding desertion to arms theft, probably had decided that Fort Yuma was going to become a little too warm for him.

Upon reaching Tucson, the volunteers, along with other reinforcements, prepared to ride south to join Crabb. The filibustering bubble burst, however, when they received ominous news from Sonora.[9]

Crabb, meanwhile, held a council of war with his forty-four survivors. They were out of food and water and had only a few rounds of ammunition. To continue fighting meant certain death. The "governor" advised surrender. Not surprisingly, a few of the men objected. They had vivid memories of both the Alamo and the Mier Expedition. In the latter, troops surrendering to Mexicans had been decimated. But now those who favored surrender carried the day.

A white handkerchief was attached to a ramrod, and at 10:30 P.M. on April 6, Crabb limped out to the courtyard. The weary survivors were led into the plaza, and their hands were bound behind their backs. Then they were taken to a temporary barracks on the church grounds, where they spent a fearful night.

At dawn the men were marched to the churchyard cemetery. There they were told that they would be executed immediately. In groups of ten, the men were lined up with their backs toward the firing squad. One cursing filibuster screamed, "You are afraid to face us," as a volley cut him down. As the last group was led out, Gabilondo stepped forward. Addressing a frail, baby-faced lad in the group, he asked, "How old are you?"

"Fifteen," the boy answered.

"Spare him" was the curt command from the Mexican colonel.

The rest were shot. All except Crabb. As the officer in charge of the execution squad beckoned to him, Crabb requested pen and paper and a few moments. The request was granted, and the "governor" wrote a last, loving message to his wife. He laid down the pen and strode erectly before the firing squad. A volley was fired, and Crabb joined his men in death.

While Crabb's men were meeting their fate, reinforcements under Captain McKinney, approaching Caborca, ran into a hornets' nest of Mexican lancers. McKinney's men, after stopping charges by the Mexican cavalry, finally broke and scattered into the brush. After many close brushes with quick death at the end of a Mexican lance, twenty-one of the men fought their way back through the more than one hundred miles of desert to the American border.

Another Mexican troop crossed the border to strike at the camp at Sonoita, where the sick and injured had been left behind. There four men were found and shot by the Mexicans; and Jesus Aiensa, Crabb's brother-in-law, was captured and taken away to a long imprisonment in Mexico.

As Clint Thompson, Dutch, and other volunteers were riding south, an excited rider rode up to the group and reported the disaster. After Crabb was shot, he said, his head was severed with a saber stroke and dragged through the streets of Caborca. The head later was immersed in a keg of mescal, the fiery Mexican liquor, and sent to Mexico City in mute testimony to the victory over the buccaneers.

After several days of imprisonment, fifteen-year-old Charles Edward Evans was freed. Perhaps as a warning to would-be filibusters still lurking in California, he was taken back to the execution ground. There he saw that the unburied bodies of Crabb's army had been left as fodder for the hogs. Glancing contemptuously at the half-eaten corpses, a villager told the boy, "They will make our hogs fat." Charles got the point. Upon returning to the United States, he never again let idle dreams of land and glory tempt him across the border.[10]

After Crabb's demise, Dutch worked as a teamster hauling supplies along the Arizona trails. In late summer of 1857, he again was camped near Maricopa Wells. In 1857, Maricopa Wells had become a key stage station on the short-lived San Antonio and San Diego Mail. The line became best known as the "Jackass Mail," because it ran over roads so rough that it was said they could be traversed only by a jackass. A California newsman once said that the line ran "from no place through nothing to nowhere."

On the morning of September 1, 1857, Dutch and his companions saw large clouds of dust and heard the sharp echoes of gunfire about five miles from camp. Dutch recalled, "The Penrow [*sic*] (probably the Pima) and the Maracopo [*sic*] Indians were returning from a big fight they had with the Helapocho [*sic*] Indians. When we passed the battleground we saw a great many dead horses."[11]

What Dutch heard and saw that morning was a pitched battle between warring Indian tribes who lived along the Gila and Colorado rivers. The Quechen, better known as the Yumas, allied with Mohaves, Yavapais, and Tonto Apaches, had attacked several Maricopa Indian villages just before dawn.

The Maricopas were spread out in more than a dozen villages along the banks of the Gila River near the wells. They cultivated hundreds of small irrigated fields, where they raised corn, wheat, beans, squash, melons, and cotton. Their hereditary enemies, the Yumas and their allies, lived mostly along the banks of the Colorado River to the northwest. The two groups had raided, raped, and looted each other for generations. This time the Yumas organized a massive raid designed to take the Maricopas by surprise and decimate their strung-out encampments.

At their rendezvous on the Colorado, hundreds of the raiders assembled and began a nine-day march on foot across the desert, through a wilderness of rock, sand, creosote bush, and cactus. After traveling more than 160 miles, they reached a strand of cottonwood trees that lined the arroyos just behind the Maricopa villages.

Huddled there under cover of night, they prepared for the morning battle. The Yumas carefully painted their faces jet black and the rest of their bodies bright red. They wove feathers into their long hair and wrapped sashes of red calico around their waists. The Yavapai stripped to their breechcloths. There were few firearms. Most of the raiders were armed with war clubs, bows and arrows, and lances. Shortly before dawn, on September 1, they charged out of their cover and, screaming shrill war cries, descended upon their still-sleeping enemies.[12]

Isaiah Woods, the new manager of the San Antonio and San Diego Mail Line, with several other expressmen, was camped near the wells eating breakfast when the group saw a burst of flame shoot up in the north. It was soon joined by other fires, until smoke covered the horizon. Then Woods saw the Yuma raiders hurling torches onto the brush-built homes of the Maricopas. He heard loud screams and saw men, women, and children running wildly, as the pursuing raiders clubbed them to the ground and smashed their skulls with their heavy war clubs.

Suddenly a horse bearing a gray-haired rider galloped up to the Americans.[13] In a letter to the postmaster general of the United States, Woods wrote, "One aged chief, whose wife had been killed by the Yumas, rode furiously up to our camp, foaming at the mouth, and begged us in good Spanish to aid them against the Yumas." With more discretion than valor, Woods said, "Of course we refused."[14]

After the surviving Maricopas had fled into the desert, the looting began. Seizing supplies of corn and melons, the Mojaves and most of the other Yuma allies gathered their loot and, leaving the scene of the carnage, began their long trek homeward. The Yumas, however, continued to loiter around the burned settlements, apparently congratulating themselves on their victory. It was a fatal mistake.

The untouched Maricopa villages further to the south, now aware of the raid, quickly rallied. In all the Gila settlements, warriors grabbed weapons, mounted horses, and galloped to the scene of the massacre. Bursting from a strand of mesquite, hundreds of furious Maricopas rode down upon the invaders. The Yumas, caught off guard and exhausted from their long march and the fury of their own attack, were able to offer little resistance. The fight turned into a slaughter, and only a few Yumas escaped death at the lances and war clubs of the vengeful Maricopas by fleeing into the nearby mountains.

An American, John Hinton, who viewed the battleground, wrote, "We found ninety corpses lying in one spot." One of the station agents left at the wells later reported, "We counted fifty-five dead Yumas along the road, pierced full of arrows."[15]

Historians Clifton B. Kroeber and Bernard L. Fontana wrote that the battle "was the end of an epoch in the history of humankind. . . . No mere raid, it was an episode of warfare. There were at least four hundred men involved—some say as many as two thousand—and casualties ran high."[16] What Isaiah Woods and Dutch Wurzbach had observed was the last major battle of Indians with other Indians in the Southwest. Indeed, an era had ended.

CHAPTER 5

Mining, Mormons, and Matilda

Crabb's debacle notwithstanding, Dutch had not yet had his fill of adventuring into Mexico. At loose ends back in Tucson, he met a diminutive, mysterious man who would give his name only as Jacob. Jacob claimed to be one of the survivors among the reinforcements who had fought their way back from Caborca.

He regaled an attentive and possibly still naïve Dutch—who was, after all, only nineteen years old—with stories about his secret knowledge of gold mines in Sonora. Dutch later remembered, "He took a great liking to me . . . and if I would get five or six men he would take us there." Jacob spoke fluent Spanish, German, and English and claimed to have friends among the Mexican officers in the area around the Santa Cruz River just south of the border.

Dutch, with youthful enthusiasm, cajoled five of his friends into forming "a company," with Jacob as guide. With his usual disdain for responsibility, Dutch got a "young man named William Tucker" named captain. "We were all young men," he explained, "and looking for an advantage."[1]

In high spirits and sure of finding enough gold to make them rich for life, the little band left Tucson and headed south along the banks of the narrow and sometimes dry Santa Cruz River. As they were riding south, Jacob told Dutch about two wild men who had lived thirty years in the ruins of the abandoned Spanish mission at Tumacacori, about forty miles south of Tucson. They were so wild and crazy, Jacob said, that the Mexicans, and even the Apaches, were superstitiously afraid of them.

Dutch always was ready, in the vernacular of the day, "to see the varmint" and persuaded Jacob to take them to the old mission. When they arrived there, Dutch recalled later:

> We found the two men, they were not wild; one of them was crazy, the other one had a little mind left. This mission had a wall around it, inside of the wall was about four acres. The main building and the tower had caved in, but there remained one low wing, which was alright, that was where the two men lived. They had a small bunch of goats and a large garden. The old ruins were grown over with fine grapes. They lived on dried grapes and goat meat and their clothing was goat skin.
>
> There was a fine spring of water inside of the wall and run under the wall to the outside where we camped. The wall was ten feet high and had but one small door, and the two men had big rocks to fit the door and we could not get in by the door, so we cut a small tree and lent [*sic*] it against the wall. I got on the wall and called to them but they would not come near me, at last one of them called out in German "get away from there," then I told them I was a German and a friend.
>
> They could not understand anything but the German language. After I spoke to them in German they came and opened the door for us. We stayed with them two days. I had a long talk with the one that had a little mind left, I asked him where

> they came from and how they got to that place, he told me that he and his brother ran away from a German ship and was afraid of being caught, and that they traveled for a good many days, he did not know how far they went nor where they were, that they had to starve so long that his brother went crazy.
>
> They were afraid to go to any settlement for fear they would be caught, they found that old mission and stayed there. He told me that they had lived there for thirty years, and that we were the first persons that they had let inside of the walls, that I was the first person that had talked German to him. They gave us dried grapes and killed a goat for us and gave us fresh fruit from their garden and they would not take any money. I don't think they knew what money was.[2]

Having seen the wild Germans, the little troupe continued down the Santa Cruz a few miles until they reached an old mission at Calabazas.[3] There, the Dragoons they had dropped off at Tucson while on their way to Fort Yuma had established Fort Buchanan.

Calabazas (the word signifies *pumpkins*) lay ten miles north of present-day Nogales and originally was a Pima Indian pueblo. Toward the end of the seventeenth century, Father Eusebio Kino, the Jesuit explorer, had established a small settlement there; but, like the other Arizona missions, it could not withstand the continual raids of the Apaches and was abandoned. Early in the nineteenth century, Calabazas was a stock farm supplying the mission at Tumacacori. The Spanish kept the Apaches under some degree of control during those years by providing them with generous food rations. When Mexico secured its independence, the young government—wracked by continuing revolts and political anarchy and close to bankruptcy—ceased placating the Apaches and stopped providing rations. Immediately the tribe starting raiding.

In 1853, the Sonoran *jefe*, Manuel María Gándara, bought the land and began to raise sheep and goats there. He converted the old church into a ranch headquarters and soon was running stock by the thousands along the Santa Cruz River. The flocks quickly attracted the notice of the Apaches, and in 1854 a war party of two hundred tribesmen attacked Calabazas.

The Mexicans, however, had been forewarned of the attack and had brought in sixty Dragoons and forty allied Indians, who concealed themselves and waited for the attack of the unsuspecting Apaches. When the raiders rode in, expecting little or no resistance, the defenders rose up and blasted away, slaughtering many of them. According to an American witness, the jubilant defenders celebrated by making an elongated necklace out of Apache ears. Over the next two years, however, the Apaches continually harassed the ranch, until finally, in 1856, it was abandoned.

After renewing old friendships with the Dragoons at Fort Buchanan, Dutch and his party continued their journey to a place he called "Mission St. Lossos." There, he said, "We found plenty of grapes, pears and peaches growing wild."[4]

From there they crossed the border and followed the river upstream for a few miles, until they reached the little village of Santa Cruz. There Jacob's supposed friendship with the Mexican authorities proved a chimera, as the *comandante*, one Captain Gómez, refused the *norteños* permission to go prospecting in the nearby hills. They were told that they must acquire Mexican citizenship before mining permits could be granted by the authorities in Mexico City. Making themselves comfortable in Santa Cruz, the *gringos* filled out innumerable forms and probably paid the *comandante* a goodly sum, while awaiting approval from the far-away capital.

While Dutch and his friends were lolling about Santa Cruz one morning, a large war party of Apaches was spotted heading for the town. Captain Gómez barked orders for all the inhabitants to run to the adobe fort just outside the village. Women clutching babies, men and boys herding cows and goats, old ladies holding bedclothes and cooking utensils—all scrambled inside the adobe walls, and the wooden gate was slammed shut.

The few soldiers of the garrison manned the loopholes in the walls and waited for the Apaches to come within range. Staying outside musket range, however, the raiders began setting fire to houses in the village. Amid the prayers and wails of the villagers, one of the Americans spotted a small cannon in the fort courtyard.

The old muzzle-loader, they figured, could hit the Apaches, who were now burning and looting the entire Santa Cruz *pueblo.* The Mexican soldiers refused to use the cannon, either because they didn't know how to load and fire it or because they were afraid it would blow up. Fortunately, one of Dutch's companions was a former artilleryman named Charlie Miller. Charlie announced that he not only could operate the cannon but also could blow hell out of the raiders if Captain Gómez would give him permission to use it.

Gómez, probably in desperation, gave permission, and the Americans hauled the cannon up to the gate of the fort. Charlie found powder, projectiles, and fuses. Ramming a powder charge and shot down the muzzle, Charlie stood by the touchhole with a burning fuse and ordered, "Open the gate."

As it swung open, Dutch could see that "there was about fifty Indians in range." The Americans lugged the gun out beyond the fort's walls. Then Charlie placed the burning fuse into the touchhole, and the cannon, with a mighty blast, fired its charges into the ranks of the Apaches. Several of the latter fell dead from the cannon blast, and then "they all ran off about three hundred yards and stopped to see what had happened. . . . We loaded and gave them another shot which made them run."[5]

Dutch doesn't say what the projectiles were that they fired with such salutary effect, but it was probably some form of canister or a handful of musket balls, which, when jammed down the barrel, made the cannon, in effect, a giant shotgun.

After the Apaches had dragged off their dead and withdrawn to find easier prey among less well defended Sonoran villages, Captain Gómez treated the Americans like heroes. In gratitude, Dutch said, "the Commandante gave us papers to go anywhere we wanted to in any part of Sonora."[6]

With all the necessary papers and the blessing of Captain Gómez, Dutch and his company bought tools and provisions, and Jacob led them on the trail to the Santa Cruz mountains, where they believed they would discover fabulous amounts of gold. Arriving at Jacob's secret place, they set up camp and began digging. Surprisingly, they quickly hit pay dirt. However, as Dutch recalled:

> We found some gold in every pan full of dirt we dug, but we had to carry it a long ways to water, and we had no way of getting the fine dust gold out of the sand, all we could get was the larger grains.
>
> We prospected in the canyons and valleys but found gold only in the mountains. We stayed there until all our money was gone and we had to sell our horses to buy provisions, for the Mexicans would not take gold dust. We had gotten between twenty and thirty ounces of gold and then the water gave out and we had to get away, so we buried our tools and started for Fort Buchanan. We started across the mountains afoot and took with us what we could carry.[7]

Jacob knew the country well, but soon the wearied prospectors were half-dead from thirst. "When we got to the top of the Santa Cruz mountains . . . our Captain (William Tucker) jumped up and said, 'Well boys, we are broke and this little stuff I am carrying won't help us much . . . so here goes,' he said, and pulled out the sack that had our gold dust in it and scattered it over the mountains. We did not have a dollar left, but we got to Fort Buchanan alright anyway."[8]

When the deflated little band of bankrupt gold miners straggled into Fort Buchanan, Dutch said, "as luck would have it, I found some of my old friends." So William Tucker, the captain; Charlie Miller, the artilleryman; and Dutch, the chief dreamer of the bunch, signed up as teamsters on a supply train that was hitching up to travel to Fort Fillmore, New Mexico.[9]

The train traveled east along the wagon trail blazed by Capt. Phillip St. George Cooke and his Mormon Battalion during the War with Mexico. After crossing over the southern tail of the Rocky Mountains and entering the New Mexico territory, the wagon train, according to Dutch, picked up "two or three dead heads, who had no money." The men were allowed to join the train, and everything went well until they reached a place called Mule Spring.[10]

By this time, the train had begun to run short on food. Tempers flared quickly, and one of the teamsters got into an argument with one of the "deadheads" over the evening ration. Hot words quickly turned into a deadly fight. The teamster pulled his Bowie knife out of his belt and, with a lightning-fast thrust, slit open his opponent's stomach. As the man fell to the ground writhing in pain, Dutch said, "some of his intestines rolled out." The stricken man, who had a reputation for meanness, was without friends, according to Dutch. Moaning, he writhed on the ground begging for help but received no aid from any of the men. A touch of Good Samaritan in Dutch's character surfaced:

> So at last I went to help him . . . I put his intestines back as best I could and sewed him up the best I knew how.
>
> We carried him on to Fort Fillmore . . . when we arrived . . . we put him in the post hospital and the Post doctor told me to come around in the morning and he would show me how to sew up a wound. . . . The next morning they had the man stretched out on a board and the doctor was cutting out my stitches. He made me stand by him and showed me how to make stitches. The man got well.[11]

Dutch lingered around Fort Fillmore for six months, driving a wagon team transporting supplies for the army. Then he and his doughty artilleryman friend, Charlie Miller, decided that they were cut out to be business tycoons and opened up a saloon and mail station one mile from the fort. At that time, six companies of troops were stationed at Fort Fillmore, making it one of the larger garrisons on the frontier.

The partners called their place "Prosseta." As Dutch later recalled, "We had to fix up a nice room for the officers. They (the garrison) got paid every two months. The last payday was all in silver.

"The first day and night after payday we had no room to put our money, we had to throw it behind the counter, and when we got time, we had to take a blanket to carry it in. . . . All the silver was in Mexican dollars."[12]

If the Fort Fillmore garrison seemed in 1857 to have a penchant for booze, less than five years later it was to become notorious. Following the outbreak of the War between the States in July, 1861, Lt. Col. John Robert Baylor, a hot-tempered Texan spoiling for a fight, and a few hundred Confederate cavalrymen advanced upon Fort Fillmore and its garrison of 550 men. Included in the garrison were seven companies of the U.S. 7th Infantry Regiment, three companies of Mounted Rifles, and a howitzer battery.

The Union fort was commanded by slow-witted, incompetent Maj. Isaac Lynde, who decided to flee before Baylor could attack his fort. Ordering supplies destroyed and setting the fort on fire, Lynde and his men slunk out that night to begin a retreat toward Fort Stanton, 140 miles to the northeast. They made rapid progress during the hours of darkness, but when the July sun of the New Mexico desert rose to its zenith, the searing heat swiftly took its toll on the retreating Yankees. Later it was charged that, in their haste, the men failed to destroy a cache of medical supply whiskey. In what must have been an act of stupidity verging on madness, the soldiers filled their canteens with booze instead of water.

Major Lynde, one of the most inept officers ever to wear the Union blue, compounded the problem by failing to bring a water wagon in his train. As the desert sun beat down upon his men, Lynde saw his parched and probably drunken soldiers first straggle and then drop out on the march. Baylor later reported, "The road for five miles was lined with the fainting famished soldiers who threw down their arms as we passed and begged for water."[13]

As Baylor rounded up the staggering troops, Lynde surrendered the remainder of his 550-man force to fewer than 300 mounted Texans, without one shot having been fired. Lynde later was dismissed from the service, but a tender-hearted President Lincoln restored his rank, enabling him to retire honorably.[14]

But all that was in the future. During that heady summer and fall of 1857, although Dutch and his partner took in a lot of silver dollars, both he and Charlie became bored with frontier entrepreneurism: "About that time I heard of the Mormon War and I wanted to go, so Miller and I gave our property to a friend."[15] Just like that.

Dutch and Charlie left Fort Fillmore for San Antonio in November, 1857. To dodge any Indian bands along their route, they rode by night and slept by day, until they reached San Antonio. After staying at home only a few days, itchy-footed Dutch, with Fort Leavenworth as his destination, rode to Galveston, boarded a steamer for New Orleans, and then took a paddle-wheeler up the Mississippi. The winter passage upstream was difficult, and travelers found the river filled with ice.

On the boat, Dutch met Brig. Gen. William S. Harney, who also was headed for Fort Leavenworth.[16] The young man told this very tough Indian fighter that his brother Charles was with the Second Dragoon Regiment, ordered to take part in the expedition to Salt Lake City, and that he wished to join him.

The Mormon crisis climaxed a long, sad story of prejudice and misunderstanding that ultimately, in July, 1857, had sent Charles and his regiment from Fort Leavenworth on a twelve-hundred-mile march to Utah. The Church of Jesus Christ of Latter Day Saints had fled there in the late 1840s to escape being persecuted for their practice of polygamy. Utah was made a territory in 1850; and Brigham Young, who had led the march of the faithful to Salt Lake City, was named governor. Although Young administered the territory virtually as a Mormon fiefdom and bucked the federal government at every turn, all went forward with reasonable serenity until, in 1857, a newly elected President James Buchanan replaced Young as governor with a political crony and former Indian agent.

When the outraged Mormons announced that they would not accept the new governor, Buchanan in July ordered twenty-five hundred troops to march to Salt Lake City and enforce federal law. Charles and the Second Dragoons were part of that force. The march took four months, with Mormon militia constantly harassing the column, blockading roads, burning crops, and destroying supply wagons. On one raid the Mormons burned seventy-four wagons and ran off fourteen hundred head of cattle, considerably diminishing the army's winter larder.

The Dragoons, under the command of Col. Philip St. George Cooke, started their march late in the season. By the time they reached the Rocky Mountains, the snow was three feet deep, and the temperature one night dropped to forty-four degrees below zero. When Cooke reached Fort Bridger, in southwestern Wyoming, on November 20, one-third of his horses had died of cold, hunger, and fatigue.[17]

When the steamboat carrying Dutch and General Harney finally fought its way through the ice and reached Fort Leavenworth, the general gave Dutch a job driving one of his supply wagons. While en route to the troops already at Fort Bridger, Harney received new orders instructing him to report for duty in Kansas, where proslavery and antislavery settlers were preparing for a blood bath. Dutch drove a wagon carrying Harney back to Fort Leavenworth.

A few days after Dutch arrived there, an army officer put him in charge of a supply train hauling food and driving fresh horses and mules to the expedition forces heading for Utah.

Meanwhile, the command of the Utah Expedition had been given to Col. Albert Sidney Johnston. Johnston turned his 2nd Cavalry Regiment command over to Lt. Col. Robert E. Lee and began the journey to Fort Leavenworth. He picked up the governor of Utah who had been rejected by the Mormons and then quick-marched to join the bulk of his forces camped in the Black Hills. Reaching them on November 6, he ordered a march to Fort Bridger. The weather was "dreadfully cold," and one night "more than 500 animals perished; their frozen bodies were seen next morning around the camp."[18]

Reaching Fort Bridger, the troops holed up in a makeshift camp and tried to keep from freezing to death. After enduring a terrible winter, the snows melted and the supply trails became more passable. Johnston, now promoted to brigadier general, received enough supplies to move against the Mormons. In the first two weeks of June, he received additional troops and a hundred more wagonloads of food and ammunition. Dutch's train may well have been in this group, as he reported, "I got [there] in time to go with General Sidney Johnston and his army into Salt Lake."[19]

While Johnston was preparing for war, cooler heads in Washington, D.C., and Salt Lake City were beginning to reconcile their differences. President Buchanan appointed two commissioners, Lazarus W. Powell and the famed Texas frontiersman Ben McCulloch, to seek a peaceful settlement.

McCulloch, who had spent most of his life fighting and who previously had refused President Buchanan's offer of the governorship of Utah, seemed a strange appointment. A neighbor of Davy Crockett's when he lived in Tennessee, McCulloch had commanded part of Sam Houston's artillery at the Battle of San Jacinto, had helped smash the Comanches at Plum Creek, had raised companies of Texas Rangers all along the frontier, and, through his reconnaissance work behind enemy lines, significantly had aided Gen. Zachary Taylor's victory against the Mexican army at Buena Vista. He was one of the leaders of the proslavery, anti-Mexican secret society, the Knights of the Golden Circle. While living in California from 1849 until 1852, he probably had been an intimate of William Walker and Henry Crabb. During the Civil War, he would be made a general and would be killed in action at the Battle of Elk Horn in March, 1862. This fierce background notwithstanding, now, in 1858, he and Powell were successful in early negotiations with the Mormons.

Later, as the peace commissioners entered Salt Lake City, they were "saluted with parades, bonfires and the playing of the Star Spangled Banner." Brigham Young, the pioneering leader of the Mormons, formally acknowledged the authority of the federally appointed governor; after further concessions by the church elders, the organization on June 12 invited General Johnston to bring his army peacefully into Salt Lake City.[20]

On June 21, more than three thousand men of the federal army wended their way through Echo Canyon, the gateway to the Salt Lake Valley. Dutch described the passage:

> While going through . . . [the] canyon we could see some of the Mormons on the highest bluffs and some of their breastworks. We had to go ninety miles through the canyon. We had gone four or five days . . . when we came to a dam that had been built across the canyon to drown the army out; it was about twenty feet high; but they did not try it as they left the flood gate open. The last Mormons we saw was at the big mountain about twenty miles from Salt Lake City, it took us two days to get over the mountain. From there the whole command marched into Salt Lake City.
>
> When we got to the city we found no army there, there were a few old men, women and children, the most ragged I ever saw. Women walking the streets with old pieces of blankets wrapped around them.[21]

Johnston and his army had entered the virtually deserted Mormon city at ten o'clock on the morning on June 26. Young, being uncertain as to how the federal troops might behave, had taken the precaution of evacuating most of the population into the southern end of the Salt Lake Valley. Col. Albert G. Brackett later wrote:

> The entrance of the Army into Salt Lake City was one of the most remarkable scenes in American history. All day long the troops marched through the long streets. The only sounds which broke the stillness of the scene was the music of the military bands and the dull clanking of the baggage wagons. . . .
>
> The stillness was so profound that, during the intervals of the columns, the gurgling of the creek which runs through the city could be heard by the few who were passing silently along. It was like the city of the dead, so quiet was it.[22]

The only raucous note in the whole procession occurred when the band, passing the home of Brigham Young, struck up a ribald camp and bordello song called "One-Eyed Riley."[23]

Thus the "Mormon War" ended in a silent and bloodless anticlimax.

There were some, however who were unwilling to let it end so prosaically. Dutch wrote that, following the rather tawdry triumphal march through Salt Lake City, the army marched to Cedar Valley and established Camp Floyd, forty-five miles from the city. He recalled:

> The prettiest lake of water I ever saw was Utah Lake, we crossed the river two or three miles below the lake. While I stayed at Camp Floyd I made several trips to Utah Lake, there was a little town at the lake and the Mormons had some small sail boats . . . I got one of the men to take me out and we sailed around. . . . The water was so clear that I could see the fish swimming under us.
>
> There were eleven children at Camp Floyd that the Mormons took prisoners at the Mountain Meadow Massacre and they told us that the Mormons killed their parents and that they could show us the men.[24]

The children were survivors of the infamous massacre at Mountain Meadows, which had occurred the previous September. An immigrant wagon train headed for California had been ambushed by a band of Indians and their Mormon allies, who called themselves the "Destroying Angels." After a three-day siege, the Mormon commander promised that the 140 men, women, and children would be spared if they surrendered. They would, he said, be given refuge at the Mormon settlement at Cedar City. Foolishly, the wagon train's leaders complied. As the disarmed immigrants were being led off toward Cedar City, the Mormons opened fire, killing all the men, while their Indian allies slaughtered the women and older children with knives and hatchets. After the Mormons and Indians divided up the booty, eighteen infants and small children were spared, and the bodies of 120 victims were left to rot in the desert.

Although it was never proven that the Mormon leadership had ordered the massacre, the troops of the Utah Expedition believed all Mormons to be culpable. Aroused by the pathetic tales of the children, Dutch and about two hundred teamsters and soldiers got the names of some of the alleged perpetrators of the massacre and determined to seek vengeance. They secretly formed a vigilante band and "that night, about the time we were to start [after the guilty ones], General Johnston heard of it and had all of us put into the guardhouse."[25]

A few days later, if only to get out of the guardhouse, Dutch volunteered to take an express message to Fort Leavenworth. Along with a man named Frank Phillips, Dutch departed from Camp Floyd on October 4 and made the twelve-hundred-mile trip in the blistering time of ten days and eight hours. Dutch and his companion changed teams repeatedly: "We traveled day and night . . . We met a great many Indians, they were all going to the Black Hills. They did not bother us."[26]

After reaching Fort Leavenworth, Dutch worked as a teamster during the spring, summer, and fall of 1859:

> I stayed at Fort Leavenworth a short while and then went to Platte County, Missouri and had a fine time there sleigh riding and going to dances. After Christmas I went to St. Louis to spend the rest of the winter. While I was in St. Louis I met a Mr. Harper, a merchant and trader. . . . He employed me to take a train for his Company in the Spring. The firm name was Perry-Harper Company of Western Missouri and they wanted to get the first goods to Salt Lake City. So I went to Atchison the first of March 1859 to fit out my train.
>
> When I reported to their office Mr. Perry looked at me and said, 'You are a mighty young boy to take charge of a train,'

> but Mr. Harper told him that he had seen Mr. Wilson, the General Wagon Master at Ft. Leavenworth about me and that I was alright. So I got my orders to go to Atchison to fit out my train. I fitted up twenty-five four-mule teams and five six-mule teams and got them loaded and ready to start the 15th of March.
>
> I had a hard time the first twenty days out, but I made the trip in sixty-two days, a little over twelve hundred miles. I was snowbound for three days in the Black Hills, thirty miles from Fort Laramie.[27]

When he completed the trip, Dutch was four months past his twenty-first birthday.

Then, suffering one of his periodic (but always temporary) bouts of homesickness, Dutch and two companions, Joe and Sam Taylor, loaded two mules with supplies, mounted their horses, and set off for San Antonio. They followed the old Oregon Trail eastward, heading for Missouri, where the Taylor boys lived.

One morning, Dutch recalled, as the trio rode out on the trail, they came upon a large grizzly bear sitting in the middle of the road. Wisely they decided not to contest right-of-way with the animal and sat in their saddles while horses, mules, humans, and bear stared at each other. Finally the bear must have gotten bored and rose up and moved to the side of the road. Dutch said, "We passed very quietly."[28]

Their journey was without incident until they crossed the Rocky Mountains and began trailing downstream along the Sweetwater River in southeastern Wyoming. Near an area called Devil's Gate, they spotted Indians in the distance. The trio nudged their mounts and quickened their march, but the warriors continued to keep pace with them.

Frightened, the trio decided to make for a fortified stagecoach station (probably Sweetwater Station, a few miles east of Independence Rock), hoping to reach it before nightfall. About two miles from the station, as they passed through a narrow canyon, the Indians shouted bloodcurdling war whoops and whipped their ponies into a gallop. Dutch and his companions put the spurs to their mounts and raced out of the canyon onto open ground.

Galloping clear of the canyon walls, they spotted a line of two dozen Indians blocking their path to the station. Jerking on their reins, they came to a rearing, sliding halt. Cut off from the stage haven, they turned and galloped to the nearby bank of the Sweetwater River. "We got off our horses and tied them together and hobbled them. Then we got between the horses and the bank of the river. We intended to sell our lives as dear as we could."[29]

As the Indians rode up to within a hundred yards of the men, Dutch stepped out from behind the horses. "If they don't stop, start shooting," he told the brothers. Heart in his throat and a revolver clutched in his hand, he walked toward the Indians, holding up his other hand as a signal for them to stop.

Surprisingly, the band reined to a halt and consulted for about five minutes. Then their chief, holding a piece of paper in an outstretched hand, trotted up to Dutch. Proffering the paper, the chief smiled. Taking the letter, Dutch read aloud, "This band of Indians are friends of the whites." Dutch handed the paper back, and there were smiles all around as he shook the chief's hand. By then, whites and Indians all were grinning furiously. However, as they said on the frontier, the smiles were a mile wide and an inch deep.

Dutch turned to the Taylor brothers, whose sweating palms clutched their rifles with fatalistic determination. "Saddle up, boys," Dutch told them, "I don't think they'll trouble us here." As three very lonely white men untied their horses and mounted, the Indians "were all around us," Dutch said. They bunched up around the trio, each of whom rode with one hand on the reins and a carbine in his lap, until they got about half a mile from the stage station; then "they gave a yell and left us."

Reaching the safety of the station, the men breathed a sigh of relief, but only momentarily. The station was occupied only by the manager, his wife, and one other man. After the lady fixed them a welcome supper, they prepared to spend an uneasy night bunked down at the stage stop. Following the meal, however, the manager told them that there was no room for their animals in the station stables. He was afraid, he said, that after dark the Indians, expert horse thieves, would slip up and steal their horses and mules, which were tied up outside the station.

Reluctantly, the tired travelers decided to slip out after dark, although the woman, deathly afraid of the lurking Indians, urged them to stay. But when night fell, Dutch and his companions swiftly saddled their mounts and silently rode out about five miles and camped "at a little island in the river covered with willow brush." That night they heard nothing.

A few days later, on the trail, they were overtaken by an eastbound stagecoach that waved them to a stop and told them the sad news. Indians had attacked the station, killed the two men, rounded up all the horses and mules, and burned the cabin and stables to the ground. The woman was found lying comatose inside the stagecoach. In his delicate Victorian language, Dutch reported the Indians had "bruised the poor woman so that she died before they got her to Fort Laramie" for medical help.

Dutch and the Taylor boys joined forces with the stagecoach and its passengers and rode along the Oregon Trail with them until they all reached the safety of Fort Caspar, on the banks of the North Platte River. There Dutch looked for his brother among the Dragoon garrison and was disappointed to find that Charles had returned to Texas on a furlough. After resting a few days, the trio made the short trip to Fort Laramie.[30]

On level land near the junction of the Laramie and North Platte rivers, the high walls of Fort Laramie offered a welcome haven for emigrants heading to Salt Lake City, Oregon, and California. It was a favored stop for the Overland Stage and later for the famed Pony Express.

In 1846, during the waning days of the fur trade, historian Francis Parkman described Fort Laramie: "The little fort is built of bricks dried in the sun . . . with bastions of clay in the form of ordinary blockhouses at two of the corners. The walls are about fifteen feet high and surmounted by a slender palisade."[31]

Matilda Stowe, about 1860. This photograph was taken around the time she married "Dutch." Although often separated, the couple managed to have thirteen children, but only twelve survived. Courtesy Douglas V. Meed

It was estimated that, between May, 1850, and mid-August of that year, the fort offered protection to 39,506 men, 2,421 women, 2,609 children, and 9,927 wagons of gold seekers and settlers traveling west. During General Johnston's Utah campaign, the great freighting firm of Russell, Majors, and Waddell in 1858 employed

3,500 wagons, 40,000 oxen, 1,000 mules, and 4,000 men to haul supplies to the army.[32]

After their scrape with the Indian war party, probably Sioux, the three young men found the stout walls of Fort Laramie a welcome sight indeed.

Following a good rest in the safety of the fort, the three men continued their homeward journey. The two Taylor brothers turned off on the trail that led to their Missouri home; and Dutch continued alone to St. Joseph, Missouri, where he sold his horse and mule and took a train to Hannibal. There he boarded a steamer to St. Louis, changed boats, and journeyed down the Mississippi to New Orleans, where he booked passage on a coastal steamer for Powder Horn, Texas, a small port on the Gulf Coast.

"We had just gotten into the Gulf," he recounted, "when a bad storm hit us and tore one [paddle] wheel and all the bulwarks away. We were three days getting to Galveston, we had to stay there three days for repairs before we could go on to Powder Point. I got home to San Antonio the 15th day of November, 1859."[33]

In short order, said Dutch, "I wanted to go to California again but I was tired of rambling, so I stayed at home and on March the 15th, 1860, I was married to Miss Matilda Stowe. I tried farming, I did not like it very much, as it did not suit my nature, so I went on a horse ranch."[34]

Stowe, a pleasant, plump-faced woman two years older than Dutch, was from a Scotch, Irish, and English family which had immigrated to New York in the eighteenth century. Generation after generation, her ancestors had migrated west, going down the Erie Canal, pausing a generation in Ohio, and then, over the years, traveling on to Kentucky, Missouri, and finally Texas.[35]

Although Dutch gives his bride only cursory mention in his memoirs, it must have been a reasonably successful union, as the couple produced twelve children. And Matilda must have had an angelic disposition to put up with Dutch and his perennial hunger for travel and new adventures.

CHAPTER 6

Or Fight for Evermore

Into the fight we went with cheerful Hearts
Remembering what we swore
That we would live as Freemen live or fight forever more
They saw that we intended there that day to drive
them out or die
And some of our brave Heroes did fall and bleed and die

The time had come when every man who had an eye could see
Upon that awful field who a freeman wished to be
We dreaded not their whizzing bombs more than
the falling leaves
We were fighting for our rights
and to drive out old Lincoln's thieves.

—W. M. Oldham, Company H, 15th Texas Volunteer Infantry, written after the Battle of Bordeaux Lea, November 3, 1863

While Dutch was roaming the frontier during the 1850s, relations between the northern and southern states were deteriorating steadily, as the cancer of slavery fanned passions to a point where compromise became impossible.

In the waning days of peace, Dutch was enjoying the excitement of rounding up wild mustangs and breaking them to the saddle. He probably was only vaguely concerned with the political drama unfolding across the nation and with the unrest growing throughout Texas.

Texas was a state not noted for the politics of amiability, a place where tempers were short and passions fevered. Although only 5 percent of the four hundred thousand white Texans owned slaves, an almost universal fear existed that northern abolitionists would instigate slave rebellions. Moreover, the white population of Texas had a general aversion to the idea of social and political equality between the races.

Like Sam Houston, many Texans countenanced slavery although they personally considered it repugnant; at the same time, however, they pledged eternal loyalty to the federal Union. In a rousing campaign in 1859, Houston was elected governor of Texas after denouncing the secessionists and pledging continued support for the Union.

But Texans who believed in compromise received a frightening shock when the abolitionist madman John Brown raided a United States arsenal at Harpers Ferry, Virginia, in October, 1859. Although Brown was tried, convicted, and hanged for his actions, the abolitionists elevated him to the sanctified status of a martyred crusader. The revelation that Brown had received funds from prominent northern citizens in order to conduct a war against slavery convinced many Texans that Lincoln's election victory would lead to bloody invasions. They feared the peace would be shattered in a continuing northern effort to subvert slavery and free the Negroes.

Brown's raid was probably the single event that did most to bring those who held no slaves to support secession. Texans already had enough border problems, with Comanches to the north, Mexican bandits to the south, and Apaches to the west. The fear of adding another hostile border to the east, where vengeful slaves would be led by fanatical abolitionists, was more than they could countenance.

It was time, most believed, to sever their bonds with a Union that had not, or would not, protect them. Reluctantly, most Texans threw in their lot with the East Texas slaveholders. They believed they could, as in the past, best rely on Texans to defend the Texas homeland.

The Knights of the Golden Circle—fanatic slavers who wished not only to defend the "peculiar institution" but also to carve a greater slave empire out of Mexico and Central America—reinforced the growing hysteria with fanciful stories of plans for slave revolts and for the slaughter of white women and children. Across the state, opposition to slavery and secession was throttled; books were burned; people were flogged or even lynched. Stories of conspiracies spread like summer grassfires. During the summer of 1860, a series of strange and mysterious fires, supposedly signaling a slave uprising, was reported in North Texas.

While some evidence suggests the existence of an inept plot by a few fanatical Abolitionists to ignite a slave insurrection, the instances of arson beginning in July, 1860, and lasting through August were blown far out of proportion by the advocates of secession. Vigilance committees were organized throughout the state; their "investigations" soon produced from Negro slaves wild confessions of planned arson and rebellion.

These "confessions," whether real or coerced, were given widespread publicity by Texas newspapers, which heightened the level of paranoia by preaching violence against all moderates and Union loyalists. Although the arson scares came to an end in September, the mysterious fires provided a background of hysteria that further strengthened Texans' belief that they must be masters of their own destiny.[1]

The presidential election of 1860 became the most bitter in the history of the young nation. Abraham Lincoln, the Republican candidate, not only opposed the extension of slavery but had grimly predicted, "A house divided against itself cannot stand. I believe this government cannot endure permanently half slave and half free."[2] The prophecy was to become self-fulfilling, as the election results were borne across a dividing nation.

The Democratic party split wide open over the slavery issue, with the southern branch of the party threatening that the election of Lincoln, a "Black Republican," would result in dissolving the Union. For president, they nominated John C. Breckinridge of Kentucky, who ran on a platform supporting protection of slavery. The more conciliatory northern Democrats, who supported "popular sovereignty" and no interference with southern institutions, nominated Stephen A. Douglas of Illinois. The plantation gentry organized the Constitutional Union Party and threw its support to John Bell of Tennessee, who, supported by Sam Houston, pledged to support both slavery and fidelity to the Union.

The Democratic split, however, made the election of Lincoln inevitable. Events followed rapidly, with South Carolina seceding on December 20, 1860. In rapid succession, Mississippi, Florida, Alabama, Georgia, and Louisiana left the Union.

Secessionists demanded that Governor Houston call a convention to discuss Texas' departure from the Union. Upon his refusal, they, on January 28, 1861, organized a rump convention to vote on secession. After heated orations, the convention on February 1 approved, by a vast majority, an "Ordinance of Secession." It was further decreed that, on February 23, the people of Texas would vote either to approve the ordinance taking Texas out of the Union or, by rejecting it, remain a part of the United States of America.

On March 2, the convention reassembled and announced the voting returns. Secession had been approved by a popular vote of 46,129, with only 14,697 voting against it. It was now official; less than two decades after Texas had joined the Union with such great patriotic enthusiasm, the state had ruptured relations with the larger republic. As war seemed imminent, the state immediately joined the Confederacy.

Sam Houston, whose allegiance to the Union never faltered, was removed from office by the convention. In a crisis of conscience, Houston refused a generalship in the Union army and, choosing neither to fight nor to oppose his fellow Texans, retired to his farm at Huntsville.

On April 12, 1861, Confederate gun batteries in Charleston harbor opened fire on Fort Sumter. President Lincoln responded by calling for 75,000 volunteers to suppress the rebellion. The war was on.

Col. Robert E. Lee, at home in Virginia following his command of the Second Dragoons stationed in Texas, was offered command of the federal army. But, after great personal agony, he decided he could not draw his sword against his beloved Virginia. When Virginia seceded on April 17, 1861, he resigned his commission and offered his services to his native state.

Although pockets of opposition to secession remained in North Texas and in some of the German settlements in the Hill Country, most of the state rallied to the new Confederacy. In the February 23 referendum, however, four Texas counties with heavily German populations voted against secession. Fifty-two percent of the voters in Fayette, 96 percent in Gillespie, 97 percent in Mason, and 60 percent in Medina voted against leaving the Union. Even Bexar County, with a substantial German population in San Antonio, voted 46 percent against secession.[3]

The majority of the German immigrants in Texas, however, if not sympathetic to secession, gave tacit support to the southern cause. Some, however, held to the liberal ideals that had caused them to immigrate from Germany. Slavery was incompatible with their ideals of freedom and democracy. In their hearts they could not give their loyalty to a Confederate cause that supported human chattel slavery.

In the summer of 1862, one such group of Germans, numbering sixty-five, determined to flee the state rode for the Mexican border. They made it to the banks of the Nueces River some two hundred miles south. On the night of August 9, Confederate cavalry caught up with them. Surrounding their camp while they were sleeping, the soldiers rode into the huddled men, firing indiscriminately. No quarter was given. Nineteen were shot to death, six were trampled into bloody pulp under the hoofs of the charging horses. The remaining Germans surrendered, only to be executed by the cavalrymen.

Dutch and Charles, who had become proficient in English and had left the predominately German settlements as young boys, long had been integrated into the mainstream of Texas frontier life. They both supported the cause of Texas and the South.

Charles received his discharge from the Second Dragoons in Fort Leavenworth, Kansas, early in 1861 and returned to Texas. He promptly joined the burgeoning regiments springing to the defense of the South. Almost immediately he was commissioned a lieutenant in the Texas army and was assigned as an ordnance officer on the staff of Gen. Henry Hopkins Sibley, who was preparing to invade New Mexico and Arizona and claim them for the Confederacy.[4]

When the war began, Texas troops seized Federal arsenals and imprisoned Union soldiers throughout the state. The legislature created new militia districts, and a few state troops moved into the frontier posts now abandoned by the regular United States Army.

Dutch was still wrangling horses on a Bexar County ranch, when he and Matilda suffered an early tragedy. Their first-born son, Charles Daniel, died in infancy.[5] Shortly afterward, in August, 1861, Dutch joined the Van Dorn Mounted Rifles, headquartered at Selma, Texas. The unit was attached to the 30th Texas Brigade which was held in service in Texas for frontier defense or to repel any invasion of Texas.[6]

This was tame soldiering for a man like Dutch. Certainly, after Charles accompanied General Sibley on his ill-fated expedition in early 1862, Dutch must have had an acute attack of his usual itchy feet. But for perhaps the first time in his life, Dutch restrained his urge to "see the other side of the hill." Matilda was again pregnant, and, after the tragic loss of their first child, Dutch was determined to stay by her side until both she and their new baby were healthy and vigorous.

In January, 1862, a squalling, healthy boy, named William Emil, was born to the happy couple.[7] As Dutch waited for wife and child to grow strong, ominous news filtered back from the West. Sibley, a drunken, inept, and possibly cowardly commander, having won some early battles through the valor of his Texas soldiers, had captured Albuquerque. But, advancing toward Santa Fe, he met disaster on March 28 at the Battle of Glorieta.

Not only was the battle lost, but the entire wagon train containing the expedition's provisions was captured and burned by Federal troops. Starving, ragged, and freezing in the New Mexico mountains, the defeated band of Texans struggled southward, hoping to reach safety at the Texas border. As spring turned to summer, the forlorn troops suffered the broiling sun and aching thirst of the desert country, as they straggled homeward.

By April, Dutch's concern for his thriving wife and child ebbed, while fear for his brother's safety surged. Feeling either a call to duty or, more likely, a lust for more adventure, on April 21, 1862, Dutch joined a newly formed cavalry regiment that was recruited to head north to engage the Union armies who were consolidating their hold on Missouri and threatening to invade Arkansas.

He enlisted in Company C, a Bexar County unit commanded by Capt. John H. Duncan. The company was part of the newly formed 31st Texas Cavalry Regiment. As was customary in Texas cavalry regiments, he brought his own horse, appraised at $125, and a saddle, appraised at $25. According to Confederate Army records, he was twenty-four years old, five feet and ten inches tall, with gray eyes and dark hair.[8] Dutch was off to the wars again.[9]

The 31st Texas Cavalry Regiment was raised by Trezevant C. Hawpe, a forty-year-old businessman and politician who recruited the unit primarily from Dallas and other North Texas communities. The exceptions were companies C from Bexar County and F from Travis County.[10] If Hawpe, who was elected colonel, had few qualifications as a cavalry leader, he turned out to be a master recruiter. Referring to the new regiment, a laudatory editorial in the *Dallas Herald* reported, "The well known energy and activity of Col. Hawpe will insure its speedy and thorough organization."[11]

Not only did Hawpe send agents to San Antonio and Austin, but also he cooked up an invasion scare and placed a signed advertisement in the *Dallas Herald*, which was published in each January and February edition, demanding:

> Who Will Defend Texas? Texas and Texans Alone. Fellow Citizens, flock as soldiers to our country's standard, and we will make our enemies bite the dust.
>
> I . . . will promise to go with immediate dispatch into the army where service can be done. . . . Duty, patriotism, affection, interest, call you at once to the tented field.[12]

The patriotic fervor generated by the broadside and, probably more important, the increasingly strict enforcement of Texas' draft laws, brought in the necessary number of volunteers; by mid-May, Dutch and a thousand like him had "jined the cavalry" for the duration of the war.

George W. Guess, a thirty-two-year-old Dallas lawyer and politician, was elected lieutenant colonel; and Frederick J. Malone, a Mexican War veteran, was named regimental major. As was customary, the recruits brought their own horses, but arms and ammunition were in short supply, and some of the men were unarmed. The troopers ran the gamut from pink-cheeked boys of fifteen to gray and grizzled frontiersmen nearing fifty.[13]

What passed for uniforms had an individual flair, not merely because of the panache of the troopers but, more importantly, because the Trans-Mississippi Department of the Confederacy was desperately short of guns, munitions, food, and boots, to say nothing of uniforms. The result was that the Texas Cavalry resembled a gang of freebooters more than it did a regular cavalry troop.

Dress included footwear ranging from deerskin moccasins to high-heeled boots, woolen pants of indeterminate color (an exception was a captain in the Lane Rangers, who wore leopardskin slacks), and gray cotton shirts with long sleeves and high necks. Hats ranged from the cowboy's wide-brimmed felt to the vaquero's *sombrero*, with a few French-style *kepis* salting the officers' wardrobes.[14]

In the early days of the war, food was plentiful enough; the main shortage was of weapons. In February, 1861, even before hostilities broke out at Fort Sumter, tough old Ben McCulloch rounded up a band of men who became part of the newly formed Army of Texas.

Lt. Col. George W. Guess commanded the Texas 31st Cavalry Regiment. He was "captured" by a beaten, retreating Union army, thus avoiding a court-martial.

With these stalwarts, Ben, on the cold, windy, wet morning of February 19, surrounded the Alamo, now used by the U.S. Army as a storage depot full of arms and ammunition. The surprised commander surrendered without firing a shot, and Texas had secured badly needed arms—but not nearly enough of them.

Units such as Terry's Texas Ranger Regiment required each volunteer to furnish his own weapon. A pair of six-guns and a twin-barreled shotgun were the preferred arms.[15] It was probably the same for Dutch's regiment, but by then, with an acute shortage of guns of all sorts, recruiters probably hoped that conscripts would report armed, rather than demanding that they do so.

On April 21, Dutch, along with the rest of Captain Duncan's C Company, was sworn into Confederate service for the duration of the war. It was not a frivolous ceremony. One of the men, who signed only his initials, "JDH," wrote that the "Company was mustered in, or as one of them expressed it, were cussed in, without murmuring." All, he said, "felt solemnity" on that occasion. "In taking the oath," he wrote, "they were bidding, probably a final farewell to many beloved ones. How many thought I, as I glanced along the ranks of these hearty hale fellows . . . shall return to their homes."[16]

These Texans were not imbued with the exuberant, sometimes even festive, mien that characterized volunteers in some of the more southern states as they prepared for war. Perhaps because of the nearness and the rawness of the frontier, they knew military expeditions to be less than romantic undertakings. As frontiersmen, they knew that their companions in the coming fray would be not hurrahs and glory, but hardship and violent death.

Perhaps the men's lack of enthusiasm was due to a year of fighting with ever-increasing casualties. Perhaps San Antonio had few black bondsmen, and slavery was not an economic necessity. Or perhaps some of the Germans' liberal idealism had rubbed off on even the Anglo population. But if they were not very enthusiastic, many were as determined as JDH, who, philosophical about the shortness of life, wrote, "To die in a good cause is all that we should desire. All of us feel we can whip the Yanks when we meet them, at least we shall do our best to thrash them."[17]

Like many educated men of the day, he expressed his emotions in poetry, which, if sometimes cloying and maudlin, nevertheless was sincere. JDH wrote:

'Tis not for gold and glory now
We go to meet the coming foe. . . .
Our happy homes we leave behind. . . .
We gave farewells, as though we should not meet
Until we met beyond the grave . . .
The foe shall find that Texans have
Unerring aim and steady nerve.[18]

With such sober thought, in early May, 1862, Dutch embraced Matilda, kissed his infant son William Emil, and swung into the saddle. Amid forced smiles and tears, Captain Duncan led Company C away from homes and loved ones and onto the road to Dallas, where the troop would join the remainder of the regiment. As the men rode off, heads turned for another longing look at their heartsick, if proud, families and friends. For many who never returned, it was their last look.[19] The march to Dallas was uneventful, except for a measles outbreak which left several of the men behind in the care of kindly farmers along the route.[20]

By the middle of May, all units of the regiment were present and ready for duty in Dallas. On May 17, the citizens of that city held a picnic for the delighted members of the 31st.[21]

Some of the citizens' enthusiasm may have abated, however, when, on that date, Hawpe inserted a notice in the *Dallas Herald* concerning a subject which continued to bedevil Confederates in the entire Trans-Mississippi region—lack of weapons. In the newspaper article headlined "To the People," Hawpe announced: "[Given] the inability of the government to furnish my regiment with arms, I have been compelled to take preemptory measures to secure arms for my men. . . . A Committee has been selected from our best citizens to provide the arms required to protect the home front from insurrections." Other arms, he stated, would be appraised and paid for. The announcement further advised, "Citizens who prefer to furnish any particular soldier with their gun can have the privilege of doing so, as guns to shoot the Yankees with, is what we want. The above explanation I deem both proper and due the public."[22]

How many weapons Dutch and his comrades purchased, exhorted, or confiscated from the citizens of Dallas is not known. The *Dallas Herald*—which, in its enthusiasm for "the Cause," made Pollyanna look like a wild-eyed pessimist—took off on another tangent. In one story, probably written in massive ignorance of the character of mid-nineteenth-century fighting, the newspaper optimistically reported the manufacture of "murderous looking Bowie knives, which will be a very formidable weapon in the hands of resolute and fearless Texans."[23]

Against the buck and ball of rifled muskets and the round shot and canister of smooth-bore cannon, now being produced in enormous quantities by the burgeoning war industries of the North, Bowie knives perhaps would not prove quite so formidable as naïve editors had hoped.

During the first week in June, Colonel Hawpe put his troops on the march to Little Rock, Arkansas, to join up with a Confederate force which, under Col. Douglas Hancock Cooper, was preparing to invade Missouri.

"On our way," Dutch recalled, "we had a good time, we had singing and music every night. Some of the boys had violins and could play."[24] Into the night, eager young voices caroled "The Yellow Rose of Texas," "The Girl I Left Behind Me," "The Bonnie Blue Flag," and rousing choruses of "Dixie."

Some of the men from North Texas, however, were less than enthusiastic. Far removed from the East Texas cotton fields worked by slave labor and with little influence in Austin politics, their area had cast the majority of the votes against the Ordinance of Secession. Many were there because of the Texas conscription laws, rather than out of devotion to the Confederacy or a desire for a fierce fight. These were, however, a minority.

Most of the Texans had strong views about the war. Typical were the feelings of Capt. Elijah P. Petty of Walker's Texas Division who wrote to his wife:

> I am in the service of my country fighting for liberty and human rights—serving God . . . when I do meet the Yanks I will make them drink the bitter waters of dark damnation for forcing me away from the comforts of home and the loved ones there.
>
> Encourage [my children] in a bitter and unrelenting hatred to the Yankee race—They are our implacable enemies. They have invaded our country and devastated it and are continuing to do so. They have murdered our best citizens and continue to do so and all because we insist upon the inalienable right of self government and as I am in eternal hostility to them I think it but right that my children who suffer as I suffer and as my country suffers should be indoctrinated with an implacable hatred to so vile and cursed a race.[25]

Pvt. John W. Truss, Company D, 12th Texas Cavalry, voiced similar sentiments. Owner of a small farm in Central Texas, near the town of Pinoak, he wrote his wife Rebecca on October 8, 1862:

> We must look at the cause and then consider the necessity of our being separated when our country and our homes and firesides is being run over by a foe that is as destitute of humanity as the worst savage that the wide world can afford. How then can any man stay at home without lending a hand to repel this miserable unfeeling foe? I could not claim Southern soil as my home if I were not to help.
>
> Beckey, it almost breaks my heart to think of you and think that I have to be away from you so long but when I . . . see the

> ruins of houses and fields burned down I then feel the love of my country swell my heart. I also see helpless women and children left without clothing and shelter or even anyone to protect them. My blood boils for revenge. I think then if it was my own beloved wife that was thus treated by those invaders of our country. . . . They cannot stand up and fight us with even numbers like men of honor.
>
> I hear that they are invading Texas. I hope we may be ordered back if they do invade our lovely state. I do not think they can start another as mean set of men to come to Texas as they have got here. I think those are the lowest down men in the world.[26]

To a twentieth-century American, these words seem unduly harsh. But, reading Captain Petty's and Private Truss's bitter letters, one can understand why the men of the Trans-Mississippi fought for four years, despite being ill-clothed, half-shod, underequipped, greatly outnumbered, wracked by disease, without proper medical care, generally ignored by the Confederate government in Richmond, and, in the last years of the war, increasingly bereft of hope. As historian Frank E. Vandiver put it, "Afar in the Western sector, raw ragamuffins played at soldiers and had no audience to care."[27]

If most of the Texans lacked the bitterness of Captain Petty and Private Truss, they were no less dedicated to the cause. It was not for the prolongation of slavery that they fought, but for their right to determine their own destinies. This was the feeling of Charles, who fought out of a sense of duty. With Dutch, it is hard to know. In later years, he was caustic about Yankees but always in a half-humorous way, delivering his barbs with a wink and a smile. It is hard not to believe that, with him, it was just another grand adventure—at least in the beginning.[28]

As Hawpe's regiment rode in leisurely fashion across North Texas, the colonel, leaving Lieutenant Colonel Guess in command, peeled off from the column and detoured to Tyler, Texas, where, from Brig. Gen. Henry E. McCulloch, Ben's brother, he picked up the enlistment bounty owed to volunteers.[29]

Guess, in a letter, reported, "The health of the Regiment is very good with the exception of one severe case of measles. . . . Weather is warm and dry. . . . We have plenty of beef, bacon and bread to eat, and have no right to complain."[30]

Colonel Hawpe rejoined the regiment in Bowie County, near the Arkansas border, and distributed the bounty money to his troopers. Then, on July 5, they crossed the Red River into Arkansas. En route to Little Rock, the regiment, lacking raincoats and tents, got thoroughly soaked. They arrived at that city on July 18, considerably dampened but in good spirits.[31]

There, the 31st was brigaded with the 22nd and the 34th Texas Cavalry regiments, which would fight side by side throughout the war. Both the latter regiments were North Texas units of varying degrees of dedication to the Confederacy. The 22nd had been recruited mostly from Fannin, Grayson, and Collin counties.[32] The 34th was composed mostly of poor farm boys from the Caney Creek area of Grayson County. Their horses were of such quality as to have the unit immediately dubbed "The Plow Horse Cavalry" by better mounted units.[33] All three regiments were placed under the command of Col. Douglas H. Cooper, a former Indian agent, Indian fighter, and veteran of the Mexican War.[34]

Overall command of the Trans-Mississippi District, encompassing the states of Missouri, Arkansas, and Louisiana north of the Red River, as well as the Indian Territory, was vested in Maj. Gen. Thomas C. Hindman. Hindman, standing five feet and one inch tall, looked like a toy soldier. His dress and lack of military bearing made him even less impressive. With no previous military experience, the lawyer and former congressman arrived to inspect his new command wearing a ruffled shirt, rose gloves, and patent leather boots, and carrying a rattan cane.

One of his felt boots was jacked up with a high heel to steady him, since his left leg was shorter than his right. Neat and fastidious, he looked wildly out of place as the leader of the motley band of ragamuffins who constituted his command. Looks, however, were most deceiving, as Hindman proved to be a tower of strength in the disorganized Trans-Mississippi District.[35]

One of Gen. Jo Shelby's Missouri troopers had pointed out accurately that the Trans-Mississippi District was "the military Botany Bay of the Confederate States, commanded continually, except when Hindman was over it, by generals relieved from duty in Virginia because of their ignorance and unfitness for any position whatever."[36]

Only four months earlier, on March 7 and 8, at Pea Ridge near the Arkansas-Missouri border, the Confederates had suffered a stinging defeat which cost them the state of Missouri and the life of that tenacious Texas fighter, Ben McCulloch. In the wake of this debacle, Hindman busily was mounting a force to reenter Missouri and retrieve that state for the Confederacy.

Although regular Confederate forces fled Missouri after Pea Ridge, that state by no means was pacified. In fact, the withdrawal of regular troops left hatreds stewing. The violence between slavers and abolitionists in the 1850s, which had turned neighbor against neighbor in an orgy of burning and killing, now left the state open to still further savaging. Guerrilla bands—under Capt. William C. Quantrill, "Bloody Billy" Anderson, and others, accompanied by teen-aged killers like the James and Younger brothers—burned, robbed, and killed in vicious raids, in which mercy was neither given nor expected.

While the Confederate forces refused to recognize many of these night riders as legitimate soldiers of the South, the southerners undoubtedly were grateful that the barbarous raiding tied up thousands of Yankee soldiers.

When such brutal irregulars were captured by Federal troops, the latter were merciless, too, in dealing with them. Typical was the report of Maj. Frank J. White, 2nd Battalion Missouri Cavalry (Militia), who attacked a band of "bushwhackers" near Eureka, Missouri, in September, 1862. As Union troops burst into the guerrilla camp, Major White reported, they found that "a man of advanced years had been taken by them the night previous. A rope was put around his neck for the purpose of hanging him, but the bushwhackers were frightened away. . . . Captain Nevins was captured in the vicinity of Eureka with arms upon his person. He wore a mask when captured. . . . I ordered a drum-head court-marshal . . . and [he] was condemned to be shot to death."[37]

White reported that he had all southern sympathizers in the area brought to his camp "in order that they might witness the execution. . . . At noon of the 24th the sentence was carried into effect and the house of the prisoner burned to the ground . . . I was in a section of the country where a perfect reign of terror had been instituted by the lawless marauders lurking in the bush . . . I ordered all the houses belonging to men of Captain Nevins' gang to be burned to ashes."[38]

The cycle of murderous raids and summary executions never seemed to end. Maj. A. T. Denny, at Headquarters, Northeast Missouri Division, wrote orders to a subordinate outlining in precise detail "with due form and ceremony" how he should parade his command and march to the execution ground and select six-man execution squads for each prisoner to be shot. One rifle in each six was to be loaded with a blank; the prisoners were to be "blindfolded and made to kneel before the firing party;" and the execution was to be carried out. Sometimes a dozen men were executed at the same time.[39] While Grant and Lee in the East fought while observing civilized proprieties, in backwoods Missouri it was war to the death.

Looting was endemic. But if you were caught, the price was high. A Confederate cavalryman described one such incident: "We caught sight of two men [Federal soldiers] coming out of a burning house, loaded with plunder. We took after them . . . but they did not escape. They were shot down, and no questions asked, and left where they fell, to bleed and die among numerous other animals."[40]

While his regiment rested in Little Rock, Dutch probably learned the good news that brother Charles had survived the harrowing thousand-mile retreat of General Sibley's doomed army, which fled from northern New Mexico all the way back to San Antonio. The battered survivors, including Lt. Charles Wurzbach, reached San Antonio in midsummer with little more than the ragged clothes on their backs. The important thing to Dutch, however, was that his older brother had lived to fight again another day.

In July the Texans rode north, toward the Boston Mountains. Colonel Cooper ordered them to leave wagons and other baggage behind and to take only that which could be carried on their horses. On July 17, it started to rain, and Dutch and his companions soon were sopping wet. They were, however, "in good humor, for they [were] whistling, singing and passing jokes with one another."[41]

Cooper's command included a regiment of Choctaw and Chickasaw Indians, as well as Col. Stand Watie's mixed-blood Cherokee Regiment. The Indians were under a cloud somewhat because, at Pea Ridge, they accurately had been accused of scalping, tomahawking, and otherwise butchering both wounded and dead Federal soldiers. Like Quantrill's cutthroats, they were useful, however, and the charges were ignored by the Confederate command.

Neither side had a monopoly on barbarism. A Confederate cavalry trooper, John Edwards, reported that, when his band overran a camp of Pin Indians fighting on the side of the Union,

> a dozen or more of the scalps of their white victims were found . . . one, a woman's, was particularly noticed. The long, soft hair had still its silken gloss, though tangled all amid the curls were clotted drops of blood.
>
> Everywhere amid the brushwood a silent scene of killing was enacted, none [of the captured Indians] praying for mercy, well knowing that their own previous atrocities had forfeited it. . . . This band of 250 savages was exterminated almost completely.[42]

Fighting between the Unionist Pins and Gen. Stand Watie's mixed-blood Cherokees was particularly ferocious, since the Pins were full-blood Cherokees who received their name from a distinctive badge worn on their uniforms.[43] To Dutch, who had grown up fighting

Comanches, Apaches, and other hostiles, the Confederate Indian troops must have seemed like strange allies.

The Arkansas-Missouri theater was weird in many respects. Maj. Buck Walton was with a band of Texas cavalrymen near White River, Arkansas, when they were startled by an apparition from the past. Bursting out of the woods came a charging troop of horsemen waving sabers and wearing suits of armor. Blinking their eyes in amazement, the cavalrymen finally realized that these were not Connecticut Yankees who had strayed from King Arthur's Court, but Union cavalry. Buck Walton related:

> The enemy wore steel breastplates that covered the man's body from the neck to the thighs. They were crudely made and held the men so stiff and straight . . . they could not control their horses. . . . They rolled and tumbled off their horses like kegs of beer or sacks of malt—and rattled when they fell. Our boys . . . killed nearly the whole party . . . many of them had these breastplates [made from] troughs, which they used for feeding their horses. It [was] not effective for protection against the force of improved rifles—but it was fair protection [from] shotguns.[44]

The sight of these ungainly cavaliers falling out of the saddle would have been laughable, had it not been so tragic. Walton did not identify the unit, but one may surmise that it was a half-trained militia unit trying to cheat death on the battlefield. In Arkansas that year, death was not so easily cheated.

In August, things were still going well for Dutch's 31st. Capt. W. W. Peak wrote that they were poised to drive into Missouri; health was "good and the regiment has been blessed with plenty of provisions for both man and horse."[45] But within days, things took a turn for the worse, as Peak reported a measles epidemic that killed one man and left many ill.[46]

In early fall, Cooper led his troops across the rugged Boston Mountains which straddled the Arkansas-Missouri border and continued marching north. The northwestern Arkansas landscape was one foreign to many of Dutch's fellow troopers, with sharply upthrust mountains, cliffs, and gorges. One Texan commented that it was "the most rugged and worthless country I have ever seen."[47]

Their march continued without incident, except when a probing Yankee cavalry detachment cut off a Confederate mule train loaded with ammunition and captured Colonel Clarkson and about fifteen men. Lieutenant Colonel Guess explained the disaster, stating, "He [Colonel Clarkson] was drunk and did not know what he was doing."[48] It was, sadly, not an unusual occurrence in both armies.

But not all officers and men overindulged in the grape. In a letter back home, Lieutenant Colonel Guess described the typical campsite where Dutch and his companions rested during the evenings: "There is no drinking in camp, not even by the Colonel. . . . This is something is it not! Hawpe went to Ft. Smith, where there is eight hundred barrels of whiskey and did not drink any at all. Hawpe is very popular . . . and deservedly so, for he leaves no stone unturned to do all for [the men] that can be done by anybody."[49]

As the jaunty Texans rode through the Arkansas and southwestern Missouri towns, ladies and young girls lined the streets waving southern flags and fluttering handkerchiefs, and Dutch and the young troopers responded with hearty Rebel yells.[50]

Through August and early September, the two armies felt each other out in southwestern Missouri like cautious and unsure boxers. Both sides engaged in multiple false alarms, interspersed with a few flurries of pickets' firing on their own patrols.

At 8 A.M. on September 20, 1862, at Shirley's Ford on Spring River, west of Carthage, Missouri, Dutch's 31st and detachments of the 34th Cavalry received their baptism by fire. Early on a cool morning, while Yankee sentries dozed, the Texans, undetected, crept up on the picket line of the Second Indian Home Guard, a Kansas unit, until they were within point-blank range. Then they opened fire. The attack started a general panic in the Union encampment, where fifteen hundred civilians were crowded in with the soldiers. As the Federals fled screaming, Texans galloped "war whooping" into the camp. Some of the men dismounted and began looting supply wagons, while others set the camp afire.

Col. John Richie, the Union commander, finally got his troops under control, brought up new units, and led them into a ravine, where they repulsed a second attack by the Texans. With reinforcements, Richie launched a combined infantry and cavalry attack. The Texans gathered up their loot and, in the words of Col. Richie, "skedaddled," leaving behind the burned camp and "12 to 20" dead Union soldiers.[51]

An interesting aspect of this battle was the report that, during the fighting, "Alfred," a black slave and personal servant of Colonel Hawpe, killed two of the Union Indians. Another "boy," a slave of Lieutenant Colonel Guess, killed an Indian trooper.[52] Whether these slaves accompanying their masters would have been permitted to fire on white troops was not mentioned.

To Dutch, the engagement must have seemed not much different from any Indian fight that occurred on the Texas frontier. His regiment had yet to encounter white troops—the real Yankee foe. It was an experience that would not be long postponed.

After withdrawing from Shirley's Ford, Cooper's command, now brigaded with Col. Jo Shelby's Missouri cavalry, went into camp at the little town of Scott's Mill. On September 22, in the neighboring 34th Regiment, a man came down with typhoid fever and "was sick five or six days and out of his head two days before he died."[53]

General Hindman meanwhile assembled a force of twenty thousand and, intent on advancing north, sent Cooper's units as advance guard on a probe into Missouri. It was a bizarre-looking force, consisting of the Choctaw and Chickasaw Regiment, some wearing war bonnets and feathers; the now ragged Texans; Jo Shelby, wearing a slouch hat with brim turned up and sprouting a long black plume, leading his hard-nosed Missouri raiders; and Stand Watie's half-breed, half-wild Cherokees. In all, Cooper had over four thousand mounted men, armed with a conglomeration of weapons ranging from bows and arrows, tomahawks, and flintlock rifles, to shotguns and some modern percussion-cap rifles captured from the Federals.

As the column pushed north, it stripped the local farms and towns of badly needed food supplies. Stopping about twenty-five miles north of the Missouri border on September 27, just a week after the affair at Shirley's Ford, the 31st was ordered to go forward and establish an outpost at Newtonia.[54] Encamping there, Cooper sent pickets to the surrounding towns in the area. All was quiet for two days.

In the meantime, Union Maj. Gen. James G. Blunt was poised to launch his own offensive, with the objective of sweeping into Arkansas and annihilating Hindman's army. He pushed out two brigades under the command of Brig. Gen. Frederick Salomon and Col. William Weer. Weer, whose pen turned out to be sharper than his brain, boasted, "The Texans are generally conscripts, and no doubt very unwilling soldiers."[55] On September 29, they made contact with the Rebels and fired on their pickets.

Early on the morning of September 30, the Union troops launched a major attack on the Newtonia encampment. Hawpe dismounted his men and ordered Dutch and his fellow Texans to take up a position behind a stone fence. Supported by a light battery of two guns, they awaited the Yankee attack. As they waited, Dutch and his comrades experienced the strain of impending combat, described by one soldier as "getting pale around the gills and swallowing imaginary frogs that would come up in his throat."[56]

The Union troops—the Ninth Wisconsin Regiment, the Sixth and Ninth Kansas regiments, and a regiment of Indian troops—launched a charge into the massed fire of the Texans and were cut to pieces. Colonel Weer later reported that "four whole companies of the Ninth Wisconsin except about ten men are killed, wounded or captured."[57]

For the first time, Dutch and his companions had killed and been killed by their white American brethren. It must have been then that the enormity of this fratricidal war was driven home to them by shot, shell, and torn and bleeding flesh.

As Cooper brought up all of his troops, the battle raged across a wide front. At one point an unidentified Confederate officer rode up to Dutch's position, cursed the Texans, called them cowards, and ordered them to come out from behind their stone wall and charge the enemy. Insulted, the Texans leaped over the wall and, screaming their banshee yell which was half Mexican *grito* and half Comanche war whoop, charged the Yankee line.

Compounding the error, Colonel Hawpe, seeing the presumed staff officer instituting a charge that he thought was ordered by Cooper, shouted for the rest of his line to charge. Texan, Missourian, Chickasaw, Choctaw, and Cherokee blundered straight into the reformed Yankee infantry and fresh batteries of artillery. They in turn were shot up badly by canister and Minié ball.[58] It was never determined who the supposed staff officer had been. Had he been found, probably the Chickasaws would have finished off what the Texans left of him.

At one point during the fighting, Cooper reported, "The First Choctaw and Chickasaw Regiment . . . entered the town at full gallop . . . singing their war songs and giving the war whoop. . . . The battle was now raging in all parts of the field, [the enemy's] masses of infantry could be plainly seen advancing in perfect order, with guns and bayonets glittering in the sun. The booming of cannon, the bursting of shells, the air filled with missiles of every description, the rattling crash of small arms, the cheering of the men, and the war whoop of our Indian allies, all combined to render the scene both grand and terrific."[59]

The fighting continued as darkness fell. Finally, the Union forces broke, abandoned their supply wagons, and in the darkness retreated twelve miles before regrouping. In all, Federal forces amounted to about eight thousand men, arrayed against Cooper's mixed bag of four thousand. The Confederates reported a loss of seventy-eight men.

For those who believe that the military-bureaucratic procedures for "covering one's arse" are twentieth-century phenomena, reading the Union accounts of this defeat is illuminating. General Salomon estimated that Cooper's ragamuffins exceeded eight thousand, while Colonel Weer reported that they numbered eleven thousand. He no longer suggested that they were "unwilling" to fight. Salomon, in his report of the battle, claimed that he "could have annihilated the enemy" if only Colonel Hall of the Fourth (Union) Missouri had followed orders and arrived on the battlefield on time. Colonel Hall, however, in his official report, claimed that Salomon "left me in utter ignorance" of his plans. He reached the "battlefield about sunset," he said, and found Union troops "retreating in great confusion."

Col. William R. Judson, of the Sixth Kansas Cavalry, reported that he saw "some ten killed and wounded who had been stripped of their clothing by the ragged rebels who left them lying naked by the side of the road." All the Union officers claimed that, though outnumbered, they nevertheless had inflicted heavy losses on the enemy. Their losses during the battle amounted to several hundred.[60] If Dutch was looking for a grand adventure, he may have gotten more than he bargained for in the little Missouri town.

The battle of Newtonia, however, proved to be the high-water mark for the Texans and their allies during the remainder of 1862. Promoted to brigadier general, Cooper and his ragged command rested near Newtonia until, on October 3, they received information that Maj. Gen. John M. Schofield, commander of Union troops in southwestern Missouri, who was thirsting to avenge the Federal defeat, was about to pounce on the Confederate camp with an overwhelming force of more than twenty thousand men. The next morning, Federal troops got within range and opened a ferocious barrage upon Newtonia.[61]

Dutch, with the 31st, held the center of the Confederate line and fought off the Federal forces until Jo Shelby's horsemen were in position to cover a general retreat. Describing the fight, Dutch said later, "Three thousand of the Yankee cavalry came charging up after us. General Cooper waited until they got within five or six hundred yards of us, then we fired a shot from our cannon into them.

"As soon as the shot was fired, General Cooper ordered the cannon linked up and had all of us to retreat. We had gotten about five miles from that place of our retreat, we could hear them bombarding the timber, and when we were 15 miles away we could not hear any more shots."[62]

During the retreat, the Texas Brigade was ordered detached from Cooper's command and put under Col. Thomas Coke Bass, another Texas lawyer turned inept cavalry commander. The brigade was retreating towards Huntsville, when General Hindman rode up on the scene. The diminutive little general found Bass "alarmed and his troops almost disorganized." Hindman quickly ordered Col. William R. Bradfute to take command. Bradfute, a Mexican War veteran, seemed an ideal commander for the Texans. He probably was known personally to Dutch, as he had served in many posts on the Texas frontier during the 1850s.

Frustrated by the disorganization of his command (the disorganization probably was due to a combination of inexperience, booze, and funk), Hindman relieved a brigadier general and a colonel for drunkenness and arrested another colonel for cowardice. Colonel Bass was arrested for "retiring without sufficient cause" but subsequently was returned to duty.[63] The Confederates, however, continued their retreat until they had crossed the Boston Mountains into Arkansas, where they planned to make a stand.

Meanwhile, the Union forces advanced under Brig. Gen. James G. Blunt, a thirty-six-year-old Kansan who once had practiced medicine in Ohio. Leading the First Division of Schofield's army, Blunt's troops managed to get close to a detachment of Cooper's Indians—who were bivouacking at Fort Wayne, near Maysville, Arkansas—without being seen. Blunt, who was as good a con artist as he was a soldier, slipped up on a fine mansion house near the Indian camp, disguised as a lost Confederate soldier. Oozing charm, he conned the resident Rebel belle into telling him the location of Cooper and Stand Watie's headquarters. At dawn the following morning, he attacked, broke the Confederate line, and drove them into a pell-mell retreat, after capturing all their artillery.[64]

The Texas Brigade, still composed of the 20th, 22nd, 31st, and 34th Cavalry regiments, continued their retreat. Dutch described it:

> We kept up our retreat until we got to the Arkansas River. My company was the rear guard all the way on the retreat.

> The first time the Yankees' advance guard caught up with us was on White River early one morning. We were just getting our breakfast. For the first time we had gotten some flour to make bread. There was twelve of us detailed to rear picket duty under Lieutenant Hale and Sergeant Beitle. We had just built a fire to get breakfast and Sergeant Beitle was making dough and putting biscuit in the skillet when the Yankees run into our two pickets and opened fire. We had to get on our horses and leave from there.
>
> We retreated to the Arkansas River near Van Buren. All during the year 1862 we had a hard time. We were kept in our saddles most of the time. . . . We were put as advance guard on the march and as rear guard on the retreat. We had a great many picket skirmishes and kept running forward and backward.
>
> After we went into camp at Van Buren we were dismounted and what horses we had left were sent home.[65]

There were precious few horses left by then, and those were half-starved and broken down by continuous marches and chronic fatigue. The men were in much the same shape. After Colonel Bradfute became ill and left his command without reporting his absence to headquarters, fiery little General Hindman finally lost patience with his Texas ragamuffins.

Col. Jesse L. Cravens was put in command of the brigade and, according to General Hindman, "since then the Texans have behaved far better than before."[66] But it was too late. With morale and discipline half-shot and horses worn out, Hindman had decided to rectify the imbalance between infantry and cavalry units from Texas and turned the brigade of born horsemen into foot-slogging infantry. The general heartlessly reported: "They are worthless as cavalry, and I have ordered them dismounted and their ponies sent to Texas. These four regiments have about men enough for two regiments of infantry." In despair over the shortages of "clothing, blankets, shoes, socks, and hats" which had left his men "destitute and in real suffering," Hindman commented bitterly on the "immense mass of wandering, unorganized and worthless cavalry that has so long cursed the country." He also referred in a report to the "infinite disorder, swindling and rascality" in the district.[67]

For Dutch, the dismounting of his regiment was a mitigated disaster, for, as he explained, "I was one of the lucky ones detailed to bring the horses home" to San Antonio.[68] The rest of the regiment was not so reconciled. With injured pride and blistering feet, the centaurs of Texas ruefully began drilling as infantrymen.

On November 22, the *Dallas Herald* reported that some of the horses of the dismounted 31st had passed through Dallas. They lauded the regiment, which, they said, had undergone arduous service, continually on forced marches, scouting expeditions, and covering retreats.[69]

Within a few days, Dutch was back in the arms of Matilda and their infant son. After months of no pay and rations that usually consisted of parched corn, home in San Antonio must have seemed like heaven. While there, Dutch probably learned that Charles now was assigned as a staff officer in the command of Gen. John B. Magruder, who was busy assembling a makeshift fleet of "Cottonclads" and a scratch infantry force with the intention of recapturing the port of Galveston.

The interlude in San Antonio was to be only a brief one, however. Before the end of the year, Dutch was back in the saddle, riding to join his regiment. It was not an uneventful leave, however, for, in the late summer of 1863, a daughter, Mary Ann, was born to the war-separated parents.[70]

Dutch rejoined the remains of his battered regiment, still headquartered in northwestern Arkansas. When he reached them, they were even more worn out than before. During the previous month, while Dutch was resting in Matilda's arms, they had fought a vicious battle at Prairie Grove, north of Van Buren, Arkansas, in which Hindman's army had suffered more than thirteen hundred casualties and again had been forced to retreat before overwhelming Federal forces.

Prairie Grove was the scene of a particular horror. Union

wounded were lying among large straw ricks when artillery shells struck the area, setting the straw afire. More than two hundred helpless men were burned to death. The scene of terror was compounded when a large herd of hogs, smelling the roasting flesh, gorged themselves on the barbecued bodies.[71] Closer to home, Dutch's company commander, Capt. John H. Duncan, "lost a leg while gallantly charging the enemy."[72]

On Christmas Eve, the Texans were hungry and freezing, their morale shattered. They finally mutinied when Bradfute, now back in command, had an altercation with one of Colonel Hawpe's orderlies and commanded that the man be punished by bucking and gagging.[73] To buck and gag a man, you tied his hands at the wrists and his feet at the ankles. You seated him on a barrel, bent him over, and pushed his arms outside his knees. Then you took a stout stick and shoved it over his bent elbows and under his knees. He was then gagged with a shirtsleeve, pants leg, or rope and left for an indeterminate number of hours.[74] The punishment was extremely painful, if not fatal; to the Texans, it was a humiliation that most freeborn frontiersmen were unwilling to accept.

Encouraged, perhaps, by a liberal dosage of Christmas spirits, Dutch and his companions, upon seeing their tortured comrade, rushed past his guard and quickly freed him. Bradfute, perhaps less judicious than usual, was enraged. He called out the guard, ordered them armed, and sent them, with bayonets fixed, into the camp of the 31st, where they seized the unfortunate orderly, returned him to his barrel, and again bucked and gagged him.

At that, the 31st went ballistic. Screaming and shouting, the regiment grabbed shotguns and muskets and, in a body, surged to brigade headquarters, roaring curses. Bradfute ordered the guard to fire upon the mutineers. They did, fortunately into the air. After much shouting, and probably through the intervention of more level-headed officers, everyone calmed down. The orderly was released, and Dutch and his friends returned to their Christmas spirits.[75] Bradfute probably was lucky that discipline held and that his Texas troops did not run amuck and lynch him.

Suffering increased throughout the winter. Conditions had been bad even as early as October, when a member of Dutch's regiment wrote to the *Dallas Herald* pleading with the citizens to send them warm clothes: "We are far, far from home . . . will our kind friends help us with clothing for the winter? I am a soldier in Col. T. C. Hawpe's cavalry in camp in the northwest corner of Arkansas. One pair of good yarn socks may prevent a soldier's feet from being frozen and save him to his country. . . . Your heart will rejoice to know you had saved one poor soldier from the pangs of the crippled."[76] Three months later, the suffering was much worse.

On January 7, the four dismounted and beaten-up Texas cavalry regiments were brigaded with the 15th Texas Infantry Regiment and were put under the command of Col. Joseph Warren Speight, a thirty-six-year-old lawyer from Waco.[77]

Marched and countermarched in freezing rain, sometimes in snow piled up almost a foot deep, and trying to live off the land in a country stripped of food supplies, the brigade was reduced—by battle deaths, rampant disease, and desertion—to less than fifteen hundred half-starved men. With the onset of cold weather and short rations, Colonel Hawpe turned command over to Lt. Col. George W. Guess and returned to Dallas. For whatever reasons, he never returned to the regiment.[78]

For this he was roundly damned by Lieutenant Colonel Guess, who with a withering pen wrote from the camp at Choctaw Station that Hawpe had left under "false pretenses." Guess charged in a letter to his close friend, Mrs. Sarah Horton Cockrell, "I understand Hawpe says he made thirty thousand dollars in two weeks after he went home. I have no doubt of it.

"By deserting his country's cause in the time of her greatest need, I care not what he says were his reasons for going home. . . . He is worse than a deserter; and I do not say this in secret. I do not ask you to keep it to yourself. It is an open and notorious fact."[79]

Undoubtedly the colonel's discretion won out over his valor during that terrible winter. What many might call the desertion of his regiment did not deter Colonel Hawpe. He continued to use his title and immediately took an active role in the commercial life of Dallas.

In February, he was chairman of a committee which selected the delegates and outlined the propositions to be sent to a currency convention to be held in Austin on February 17. During a courthouse meeting on February 5, chaired by Hawpe, the committee drafted a resolution "that we look with scorn and contempt upon any and all persons directly or indirectly, engaged in depreciating Confederate currency." Further, they demanded that restrictions on trade along the Rio Grande be ended and that "open trading" be permitted. Finally, they urged that Confederate currency be made legal tender for paying debts.[80] If Colonel Hawpe seemingly was indifferent to his freezing and starving men, he was not averse to advocating the further enrichment of Dallas cotton brokers and speculators, who were eager to ship cotton across the Mexican border, where it would be purchased eagerly by British or Yankee buyers.

Meanwhile, in a report, the new Confederate commander of the Indian Territory, Brig. Gen. William Steele, described conditions during the winter of 1862. He commented on "the exhausted condition of the country" around northwestern Arkansas and wrote of "the undisciplined, ill-equipped and demoralized state of the few troops."[81]

Arriving at Fort Smith, Arkansas, Steele reported that one regiment "had not a change of clothing nor an average of a blanket to the man." Lane's Rangers had 150 men present for duty in a "Regiment originally consisting of fourteen full companies."[82] A company at full strength consisted of 115 men.[83] Lane's regiment then had suffered more than 90 percent casualties from both battle and disease.[84] Steele stated that "about 1,500 inmates, in a wretched condition" were in the unequipped hospitals in the area.[85]

"Staff officers were incompetent and negligent," Steele reported; furthermore, "the few stores left by General Hindman on his retreat had been stolen and scattered to all parts of the country. In the Quartermaster's Department there was neither transportation or forage." There was, he said, "a very limited supply of poor beef and corn meal." The lack of rations forced General Steele to order Dutch's regiment and the other three scarecrow regiments of Colonel Speight's brigade of Texans to make a forced march to the Red River country in the vicinity of Doaksville. There he hoped they would find enough food to stave off starvation. Most of those regiments, General Steele reported, were "found to be greatly demoralized."[86]

In a further report, General Steele wrote, "Soon after my arrival [at Fort Smith] an infantry brigade was sent me, consisting of five regiments, under Colonel Speight. This brigade had present less than 2,000 men, and four of the regiments were so demoralized that it had been found necessary to distribute the men among other troops. These troops were, of course, worthless while in such condition."

Conditions in Arkansas continued to deteriorate. In addition to raids by Union cavalry stationed in Fayetteville, there were "repeated murders and robberies committed by bands of outlaws who infest both sides of the [Arkansas] river."[87]

A soldier in Dutch's brigade, Pvt. Alfred Thomas Howell, summed up the sufferings during that winter of 1862: "We were starved, nearly frozen, all the time. Our horses were only fed once in two to five days. Our men . . . suffered tremendously from diarrhea. Fort Smith and Van Buren were filled with the sick. They died by hundreds and were pushed into the ground. In this condition we fought the battle of Prairie Grove. We came back and were dismounted. Before, our starving had been a feast and our suffering the keenest enjoyment."[88]

Under these horrendous conditions, understandably, many men deserted. But if a deserter was caught, the consequences were grim. Lt. Edward W. Cade, a soft-hearted surgeon with the Texas troops, described the execution of two unfortunates:

> They were Germans from Texas. . . . The whole division was drawn up in 3 sides of a square in a field. The prisoners were marched around the enclosure formed by the troops . . .

> followed by a wagon containing their coffins. The bands were playing the dead march, they each lent [*sic*] on the arm of a Catholic priest. When they reached their graves, they knelt down and the firing party was drawn up, the command, "Ready" and "Fire" was given and both fell dead immediately. . . . My feelings were such as I never again wish to experience. One was a married man whose family consisted of a wife and 3 children. The other was a young beardless lad. . . . I can see the urgent necessity there is for rigid discipline and stern and quick punishment when the regulations are violated but my heart revolts at the idea of sending two souls young and flushed in the prime of life into eternity.[89]

In mid-January, the brigade began its march to Camp Kiamichi near Doaksville in Indian Territory (now southeastern Oklahoma), located not far from the Red River boundary with North Texas. Over swollen streams, freezing ground sometimes melted into gooey mud, the Texas scarecrows marched—or, more accurately, slowly staggered—150 miles southwest, toward Choctaw land. With little food and less forage, most of their baggage animals died. With February the snows came, making the passage even worse. Plodding, at one time, through snow eight inches deep, they finally reached Camp Kiamichi on February 8 and collapsed.[90]

Private Howell described the journey: "We lived for three weeks on cold flour and water. No tents, no blankets. . . . Many a night I slept on the frozen ground . . . with a lump of ice for a pillow." Limping on boots with holes in them, he recounted, "at night my feet swelled and I could not stand. Men died every day. They laid themselves down. They would not move and they died. . . . Our trail was a long graveyard."[91]

Lieutenant Colonel Harrison, a brigade officer who foraged some food for the men, stated, "We have been literally marched to death. We have lost more men than we should have lost in a dozen pitched battles."[92]

Some units were a little better off. Pvt. J. P. Blessington, 16th

Texas Volunteer Infantry Regiment of Walker's Texas Division, camped near Pine Bluff, Arkansas, that freezing January, and wrote how discipline was maintained in that unit:

> The morning of the eleventh . . . the Division was formed in line of battle to witness three soldiers . . . drummed out of camp for "hog stealing." The bands played the "Rogue's March" along the line. The three soldiers marched along the entire line, followed by a file of soldiers with fixed bayonets. This kind of punishment . . . seemed to be a novelty to the Texas boys and it created roars of laughter amongst the troops. Boys, ask yourselves if you were ever guilty of "hog stealing" during the late unpleasantness?[93]

Had any of Dutch's hungry companions had the good fortune to steal a hog, their company commander probably would have given them a commendation, after joining them for a rare feast. Hunkered down in Camp Kiamichi, scrounging food wherever they could, the members of the Texas Brigade were at the end of very short tethers. Measles, mumps, malaria, diarrhea, pneumonia, bronchitis, and malnutrition killed more of them than Yankee bullets.

In addition to being physically sick, the men were also heartsick, suffering that malady most destructive to morale. They began to believe that they were totally isolated and that nobody gave a damn. A major component of their despair was lack of mail from home. Colonel Guess wrote, during the winter of 1862, "I wish the cursed Post Office at Dallas . . . were sunk into the lowest depths of the bottomless pit."[94]

Trooper John W. Truss, whose 12th Cavalry stayed at Little Rock, was not much better off. He wrote on January 3, 1863, "Several of Hindman's men froze to death and hundreds of mules. Hindman's men is deserting every day."[95] But the 12th at least could take pride in the fact that it still was cavalry. The Texans of Speight's brigade, turned into foot-slogging infantry, had lost much of their élan and panache when they lost their mounts.[96]

Lt. Gen. Theophilus H. Holmes summed up the situation in a report written from Little Rock to President Jefferson Davis, when he said:

> The retreat from Northwestern Arkansas was a most disastrous affair. Out of 12,000, not more than 6,000 effectives arrived here. The remainder, in about equal parts, deserted, or were left sick or disabled. . . . My sick report, thank God, is decreasing, though it is still very large and great numbers have died. All the medical officers agree that it was owing to the diet and exposure, poor beef and cornbread being the only diet, and very many of them passed the winter without tents and scarcely with clothing to cover their nakedness.[97]

Sunk in despondency, Dutch and his scarecrow comrades suffered through the long winter. Any conviction that war was a grand adventure long ago had been converted into bitter despair.

CHAPTER 7

Battles in the Bayous

Dutch and his fellow Texans, though half-starved and more than half-frozen, survived the icy winds and frigid weather of the winter of 1862–63. On March 7, James N. Carr, a trooper in the 34th, wrote home, "Times is hard here. We draw [only] a little poor beef to eat."[1] Later in the month, however, the weather turned "quite pleasant and agreeable," as the frozen ground became "green with foliage," and the Texans were able to supplement their meager diet by fishing in nearby streams.[2]

Morale was given a needed boost when many of the men, including Colonel Speight, were given leave to visit their homes. As the climate moderated, the brigade constantly drilled as infantry at the battalion and company levels, in preparation for the coming campaign season.[3]

But if Dutch and his companions were showing splendid recuperative powers, the Texas Brigade was still a mess, according to Brig. Gen. William Steele, who was commanding the Indian Territory. On March 23, 1863, he wrote to his commanding officer: "All the Texas regiments under my command, with but one exception (Speight's), when turned over to me were utterly demoralized, and their ranks so much reduced by desertion that five regiments (including Speight's) report but an aggregate of 1,432 present."[4]

The newly appointed commander of the Trans-Mississippi District, Lt. Gen. Edmund Kirby Smith, had been warned of the conditions prevailing in his command by Confederate Secretary of War J. A. Seddon, who apprised him of "disorder, confusion and demoralization everywhere prevalent."[5]

"The army," Seddon wrote, "is stated to have dwindled, by desertion, sickness, and death, from 40,000 or 50,000 men to some 15,000 or 18,000, who are disaffected and hopeless, and are threatened with positive starvation from deficiency of mere necessities."[6]

Nevertheless, Seddon counseled the new district commander: "The most important operation in your department . . . would be . . . aiding in the defense of the lower Mississippi. . . . Plan and direct operations which will protect the valuable districts lying on the smaller rivers and bayous." In a masterpiece of unwarranted optimism, Seddon continued, "From the nature of the country and the few narrow routes that exist, as well as the breadth of the streams, I am satisfied that the whole country is among the most defensible in the world, and that comparatively few resolute, experienced men could repel hosts of invaders."[7]

It would fall to Dutch and the rest of the ragged Texans to be among those very few, very resolute men who would repel those very, very numerous hosts of invaders. The crisis came in April, when Union forces, under the command of Maj. Gen. Nathaniel P. Banks, attacked Confederate forces in southwestern Louisiana. Banks's offensive aimed to secure the west bank of the Mississippi River, in order to cut off supplies to the stronghold at Port Hudson, where Confederate troops were entrenched on the east bank. Banks also planned to overrun all of western Louisiana, which was a fertile source of cotton, rice, and sugar. Then he planned to crush the small four-thousand-man army of Maj. Gen. Richard Taylor, encamped west of New Orleans on Bayou Teche.

Taylor, a shrewd if sometimes impulsive commander, slipped

Lt. Gen. Richard Taylor, C.S.A. Outnumbered but undaunted, he vowed to fight the Union invaders if they had a million men. Courtesy Center for American History, University of Texas at Austin

from the arms of the Federal encircling movement and abandoned his Bayou Teche position. In escaping, however, he left behind badly needed supplies and a Port Hudson garrison which, from across the Mississippi, no longer could be supported.

Facing overwhelming numbers, Taylor screamed to his superior, Kirby Smith, for reinforcements. That plea marked the beginning of a long-smoldering hatred on the part of Taylor, who never could understand the problems with which the cool, cerebral commander of the Trans-Mississippi District had to contend. Threatened at many points over his vast command, Kirby Smith constantly was faced with potential Federal invasions all the way from Arkansas to the Texas Gulf Coast. The forces at his command always were deficient in numbers and in military equipment.

While the appointments of Kirby Smith and Taylor did not ease the constant bickering and recriminations that were endemic to the Trans-Mississippi command structure, at least both men were active and competent and initially had the confidence of their armies, if not of each other.

Taylor, a small, swarthy, impatient, thirty-seven-year-old man, was the son of the Mexican War hero and former president of the United States, Zachary Taylor. He had been educated at Yale, Harvard, and Edinburgh University (in Scotland). While he had no previous military experience, he was a fast learner, being promoted from colonel of a Louisiana regiment to major general after campaigning successfully in the Shenandoah Valley under the stern tutelage of "Stonewall" Jackson. Taylor had the added asset of owning a large sugar plantation in the bayou country and was familiar with every stream, bayou, ford, and market road in the area. Highly intelligent, he moved quickly and aggressively against superior forces with absolute self-confidence. He was an ideal commander to oppose the more slowly moving and cautious Banks.

At his Shreveport, Louisiana, headquarters, Kirby Smith, recognizing the Federal advance in western Louisiana as the greatest immediate peril to his command, ordered the Texas Brigade, still training in the Indian Territory, to join up with the feisty Taylor in Louisiana. After freezing in Arkansas, Missouri, and the Indian Territory, the Texans may have thought that sunny Louisiana would be a more tolerable place in which to fight. If so, they soon would be disabused of that notion.

When marching orders came in early May, Lieutenant Colonel Guess wrote of Dutch's 31st, "The boys are all in fine health and spirits and enjoy life hugely," although two hundred of them still were absent from duty and "coming in slowly" from their leaves back home to Texas.[8] Others, deserters, held out in the East Texas brush country, ignoring advertisements taken out in the *Dallas Herald* urging them to return to their duty.[9]

In good spirits, Dutch and his fellow ragamuffins marched south to Texas, then east through Clarksville, Mount Pleasant, Daingerfield, and Jefferson, reaching Kirby Smith's headquarters at Shreveport on May 14.

The commanding general, a fastidious man, was appalled as he watched the ragged Texans disembark. He reported in understandable frustration:

> Colonel Speight's brigade arrived here yesterday. He brings less than 1,400 men for duty, of which 460 are unarmed. The absentees are at their homes; they have no intention of joining their commands, and Colonel Speight reports that they can only be collected by an armed force.
>
> With the exception of Colonel Speight's regiment, and probably one other battalion [most likely this was Dutch's 31st, now reduced to battalion size], the command is an undisciplined mob; the officers as worthless as the men. . . . Colonel Speight reports them worthless, unreliable, and to some extent disloyal.[10]

The outraged general placed the 22nd and 34th regiments in camp, where they would be disciplined and drilled until they were fit to join the troops at the front. The 15th Texas Infantry (Speight's old regiment) and Dutch's 31st Texas Cavalry (Dismounted) were deemed fit enough and were ordered south to Grand Ecore to reinforce Taylor.[11]

As usual, the Texans were stripped of any camp comforts they might have managed to acquire during their home leaves, being told, "Transportation will be limited to one wagon for every 50 men, which will carry cooking utensils and ammunition only." Ordered into southern Louisiana's muggy climate during the spring rainy season, the troops were to march over terrain crawling with poisonous rattlesnakes, copperheads, and water moccasins; and with hordes of mosquitoes and other insects, of both flying and crawling varieties. Yet they were told, "You will carry only two tents to each regiment . . . exclusively for the use of the sick."[12] Within a short time, that number likely would include most of the regiment.

Resigned to sleeping on soggy ground amid rotting vegetation and smelly pools of stagnant water, Dutch and the "acceptable" Texans again boarded small steamers and sailed further south down the Red River until they reached Grand Ecore on May 19. There they camped for a week before reboarding. Sailing past Alexandria, they continued on the river until they reached Marksville, where they disembarked. From there they marched overland to Simmesport, arriving on May 30. There they camped for two weeks.[13]

The Texans took a "little getting used to" for General Taylor, who was a stickler for discipline. The general told of riding up to a Texan regiment and spotting a group of troopers crowding around a large shade tree. "The Colonel, [was] seated in the center, with a blanket spread before him, on which he was dealing the fascinating game of monte." As his commanding general made himself known, the colonel, shuffling the grimy cards, asked, "Care to take a hand, general?"

Taylor later wrote, "Learning that I would not join the sport, this worthy officer abandoned his amusement with some displeasure."

The Texans had, Taylor wrote, "No more conception of military gradations than of the celestial hierarchy of the poets."[14] The more important question, of course, was "Could they fight?" It was a question that was soon to be answered.

As in every war, soldiers careened between the terrors of battle and the numbing boredom of camp life. On rare occasions when they were paid, Dutch and his fellow Texans soon tired of playing poker with Confederate money, which, of course, was virtually worthless. A more exotic sport sometimes captured their fancy and always, unfortunately, captured their attention.

"Graybacks," or body lice, took up residence upon the sleeping Texans, as they lay amid the rotting fungus of Louisiana swamps and forests, and created an itching, scratching, shuddering hell for the men. These small companions made possible one of the more mordant camp sporting events. Lice, nestled in the hair of the chests, groins, armpits, and heads of the Texans, as well as infesting the seams of shirts, pants, and underclothes, ate away at thc usually unwashed flesh of the men, ultimately creating nasty, ulcerated, running sores, until they were plucked and squashed by vengeful fingernails.[15]

The soldiers, according to trooper Buck Walton, were amused "to catch the big ones and bet on their fighting qualities." They found "that the grown bug, when taken from the bodies of different men and placed close together, will rush at one another like bull dogs, and fight to the death." The two adversaries often were placed on the top of a wide-crowned hat, and, while cheering, half-crazed men made heavy wagers with their useless Rebel money, the two bugs fought to a bloody death.

The cleverest gambler would let a specific louse "grow and fatten on his own blood until he thought he had the most robust gladiator in camp." Then the big champion would challenge the field and, amid massive bets, enter the lists of dead heroes.[16]

If the lice were not bad enough, southwesterners like Dutch must have come close to madness when they encountered the swarms of mosquitoes that infested the watery bayou country. Even worse, as one Texan reported, was a small black bug, a snapping beetle. It would land on a sleeping soldier and crawl deep into his ear, ultimately causing the man to awake in a screaming frenzy of pain. The only defense, Dutch found, was to stuff wads of cotton in one's ears before lying down.[17]

Then there were the snakes. Unlike the deadly southwestern rattlers, who at least announced their presence by trilling their soul-chilling rattle, the water moccasins, copperheads, and timber rattlers slithered silently about, giving no warning. One Texan wrote, "Very frequently, in the swamps of Louisiana, a soldier wakes up in the morning and finds that he has a rattlesnake for a sleeping partner."[18]

Another Texan, Alfred Thomas Howell, wrote, "A large snake was within a few feet of the back of my chair with its head uplifted, looking at me and crawling towards me." Startled, Howell killed the serpent and wrote home a shaky account of the incident.[19]

The monotony of camp life was broken when Dutch and his companions skirmished with a Union gunboat and drove it off on June 3. The following day, they outdid themselves when they took on three federal warships and in turn were driven off.[20]

On June 6, the Texans joined up with a Louisiana infantry brigade under the command of Brig. Gen. Alfred Mouton. At that time, Port Hudson, one of the Confederacy's forlorn forts fronting on the Mississippi, was under desperate siege by Union troops commanded by Maj. Gen. Nathaniel Banks, the former Speaker of the U.S. House of Representatives and governor of Massachusetts. Through political influence, Banks had been turned into a blundering army commander.

The Texans were ordered to march to the relief of the beleaguered garrison, and Dutch and his companions shouldered arms and began a long hike through battered plantations and abandoned farms along narrow, dust-choked roads. Carrying everything on their backs, the shuffling Texans—boiling in the sun, soaked with sweat, shoes rotting, and making do with inadequate rations—finally came within sight of the Mississippi River.

Dutch recounted, "We had gotten within six miles of the fort." Unable to effect a crossing of the Mississippi, Dutch wrote, "We were ordered back."[21] That was fortunate, as it turned out, because, less than a month later, on July 9, the men of the Confederate garrison, half-starved, almost out of ammunition, and outnumbered more than five to one, stumbled out of their mud-filled trenches and surrendered. Had the small band of Texans managed to cross the river and reinforce the doomed garrison, Dutch might have spent the rest of the war in a Yankee prison camp. However, from a certain point of view, that might have been a blessing, given the ordeals he would face in the battles to come.

The tired Texans were ordered to march more than a hundred miles to the south, along a narrow road that paralleled Bayou Teche. The route ran through the picturesque Cajun country, where, in peacetime, fiddlers played merry tunes to intensify the gustatory delights of their gloriously unique cuisine of crawdads, fish, and vegetables, liberally sprinkled with exotic hot sauces and consumed with huge draughts of corn beer or local wine.

No such merriment enlivened this march, however, as the ragged band trudged deeper and deeper into southern Louisiana, past Washington, Opelousas, Vermilionville, New Iberia, Franklin, and Fort Bisland. The soldiers crossed the Bayou Teche and the Atchafalaya River at Brashear City on June 29 and advanced eastward to Thibodaux on the Bayou Lafourche on July 1.[22] That week, the most decisive of the war, saw the huge Confederate fortress of Vicksburg surrender to Gen. U. S. Grant, while, along a fishhook-shaped series of hills in southern Pennsylvania, Union forces under Gen. James Gordon Meade repulsed Robert E. Lee's mighty Army of Northern Virginia. The high-water mark of the Confederacy had been reached, in both the North and in the West.

One of the Texas officers wrote to his wife about summer campaigning in Louisiana: "You want to know how we live. . . . I have not eaten anything but beef and corn bread for two months . . . some times I have to force it down. . . . I am sick of war, sick of the constant contact of rough and obscene men, sick of my absence . . . from you. . . .

"The men march," he wrote, "all day through the broiling sun with the thermometer over a hundred, carrying a load of 40 pounds and suffering the intense thirst . . . caused by heat, dust, and perspiration . . . no water to drink for hours at a time. . . . I have seen a hundred fall . . . incapable of moving . . . completely exhausted from heat."[23] The heat, malaria, and bad water began to break down even those sturdy Texans who had endured the terrible Indian Territory winter and survived.

One Texan wrote of their march through Louisiana, "My division looked like a moving hospital. We had sick men in wagons and

General Banks's invading Union army crossing Vermilion Bayou in October, 1863. He again became the South's best quartermaster. Courtesy Institute of Texan Cultures, University of Texas, San Antonio, Texas

carts, wounded men on litters . . . and a crowd of enfeebled and emaciated men for whom no transportation could be had, who were straggling along."[24]

On July 18, General Taylor, fearful of being cut off, pulled his weary troops back to the Atchafalaya. There they boarded steamers and rode upriver on the Bayou Teche to Vermilionville, where they remained encamped through August. Soon, however, poor sanitary conditions, exposure, and malnourishment again took their toll; morosely, Dutch and his fellow soldiers aptly named the campground "Camp Diarrhea."[25]

In August, word filtered down that their fair-weather former commander, forty-two-year-old Col. T. C. Hawpe, who, according to the *Dallas Herald*, had been "looking in fine health" only a few months earlier, had died in an unnamed accident. One doubts that he was deeply mourned by Dutch and the rest of the dismounted troopers of the 31st.[26]

Dutch's commanding officer, Lieutenant Colonel Guess, wrote,

"We are doing nothing here but getting sick and then getting well again. When we will move no one knows." If they did receive orders to move, he lamented, they would have to leave their sick behind, because "we have no transportation." Two weeks later, on September 9, 1863, Guess reported that there were typhoid and yellow fever in the camp.[27]

The brigade's makeshift hospitals soon were overcrowded, and sick men were laid under trees without even a blanket to keep out the constant drizzle and the evening chill. To make matters worse, for two weeks the troops were inundated by a monsoonlike rain, which constantly soaked the suffering men.[28]

During this period, the brigade's commander, Colonel Speight, became ill and returned to Texas. Dutch and his fellows were put under the command of Lt. Col. James E. Harrison. That officer, concerned about his sick and dying men and with no supplies of quinine to fight off their fevers, dispatched his son to Houston, Texas, where he understood that this vital medicine could be procured.[29]

Suddenly alerted by reported moves of Union troops in their general direction, the Texans marched and countermarched to false alarms for almost two weeks. Then they returned to their old camp near Morgan's Ferry on the Atchafalaya. They had barely settled back down to camp routine when they were, on September 28, given new marching orders. This time they were not responding to Federal maneuvers; they would be on the attack.

The impetuous Texas cavalryman, Brig. Gen. Tom Green, had planned a lightning strike on an advance Federal post at Stirling's Plantation on sleepy Bayou Fordoche, about six miles west of the little town of Morganza. Green, a former Texas Ranger and the hero of Sibley's disastrous foray into New Mexico, had kept up a series of hit-and-run battles designed to keep the much larger Union forces off-balance in the bayou country.

Dutch and his friends were crowded into two flat-bottomed ferry boats and poled across the Atchafalaya in relays. They camped along the river bank and spent a sleepless night trying to keep their rifles dry during a continuous drizzling rain.[30]

A troop of cavalry was dispatched to move beyond the Yankee camp, so as to cut off any reinforcements that might come up the road from Baton Rouge. The rest of the Texas mounted men moved toward the western side of the plantation, ready to make a frontal attack on the Union positions. Dutch and the 31st, with the rest of the Texans, were ordered to march on a circuitous route to the eastern rear of the fortified camp.

At dawn the Texans set out and, slogging through swamps, sometimes knee deep in mud, along winding paths, they covered six miles until, shortly after noon, they were in position close to the enemy encampment. They crossed over a muddy levee and into a cane field. The Texas Brigade now consisted of Dutch and the 31st, which at the time was commanded by Maj. Frederick J. Malone (Lieutenant Colonel Guess was under arrest); the Fifteenth Texas Infantry Regiment; and the 11th Texas Volunteer Battalion.

As the Texans marched through the cane field, they heard firing to the west, announcing skirmishing by their cavalry. Peering out of the canebrakes, they could view the Union position, occupied by more than one thousand men of the 19th Iowa and the 26th Indiana Infantry regiments, plus two regiments of Illinois cavalry.

The Federals were barricaded in a area comprised of three sugar plantations, the Mary C. Stirling and the Abel J. Norwood properties and the Catlett Plantation. As Dutch and his fellow Texans crept through the cane fields on the northeast side of the Stirling place, they came out facing a series of buildings consisting of a sawmill, a sugar factory, and a number of slave cabins. All were filled with Union troops, now quickly alerted by the cavalry skirmishing.

Bursting from the cane about three hundred yards from the buildings, Dutch and the Texans faced "a terrible shower of whistling wounding and killing bullets."[31] As the drummers beat and the regimental flag was carried forward, the officers screamed, "Charge." Dutch and a ragged line of men broke into a run, screaming their terrible Texan yell right into the teeth of the Union fire.

Reaching a ditch, Dutch took a brief breather, until further shouts of "Charge, charge!" from their officers brought them to their feet again, to rush into the curtain of fire laid down by the increasingly desperate Union defenders. Soon, in Dutch's small company, Sgt. Maj. C. A. Beitel went down, Cpl. T. S. Jones was knocked off his feet as a Minié ball smashed his thigh, and Pvt. C. A. Whetstone, the company clerk, was struck by another bullet.[32]

Rushing helter-skelter, the regiments became hopelessly mixed up. They dashed through a potato patch and then plunged into the sugar mill and fought hand to hand until the frightened and surprised defenders fled, surrendered, or were shot or bayoneted to death.

House-to-house fighting erupted through the slave quarters, as enemy troops were flushed out with rifle butt and bayonet. Leading the Texans during this vicious fighting was Lt. John B. Jones, assistant adjutant general of Speight's Brigade. A decade later, Jones was to become famous in Texas as the leader of the famed Frontier Battalion of Texas Rangers, who, in the words of historian Walter Prescott Webb, made postwar Texas "a fairly safe place in which to live."[33]

Finally, the Federal lines broke completely, and panicked Union soldiers tried to retreat down the levee and into the woods east of the plantations. After an hour of intense, close-in fighting, the Federal troops, still on their feet, threw down their rifles and surrendered, as they were caught in the pitiless vise of the charging Texas cavalry at their front and the screaming rushes of Dutch and six hundred other Texas infantrymen crushing their rear. Only the Illinois cavalry escaped by promptly fleeing the battlefield. As the brigade commander, Lieutenant Colonel Harrison, summed up the battle, "They were whipped and running. . . . I do not think any troops have ever fought better. . . . My command was cool, steady, daring." Harrison, in the thick of the fight, was not without his own adventures, writing, "My sword was struck [with bullets] twice. I had two horses shot."[34]

In all, the 854 Federal infantry soldiers had 16 killed, 44 wounded, and more than 450 captured. In addition, General Green reported the capture of "two 10-pounder Parrott guns in fine order, with caissons complete, two new ambulances and one hospital wagon, new, filled with medical stores, and two stand of regimental colors belonging to the Nineteenth Iowa and Twenty-sixth Indiana Volunteers. Many small arms and accoutrements were saved, and every man with an inferior weapon was supplied with a good and efficient one."[35] Again the troops of Union Gen. Nathaniel Banks proved to be the best commissariat for the ragged Texas troopers.

The Texans did not get off lightly, however. Green reported twenty-six killed, eighty-five wounded, and ten missing. Praising his Texas troops, he wrote, "The heavy loss sustained by Speight's brigade shows the desperate nature of the conflict."[36]

After burying their dead in the continuing rain, Dutch and his weary companions, who had gone almost forty-eight hours without sleep, marched back toward Morgan's Ferry, reaching the banks of the Atchafalaya by seven o'clock that evening. Because of the sogginess of the banks, only one shallow-bottomed ferry could be used. The dog-tired Texans had to wait in line in the drenching rain until the next morning, when all finally made it across the river and, on the morning of September 30, stumbled into camp, bloody and exhausted but victorious.

Stirling's Plantation, as southerners called the battle, was a resounding response to the scathing criticism that had been heaped upon these half-starved, poorly equipped, mostly sick, and outnumbered Texans who had been so roundly damned by their superiors a few months before. The engagement, called the Battle of Bayou Fordoche by the Federals, was a complete, if minor, victory—a fine example of the hit-and-run tactics that General Taylor used with considerable success during the waning months of 1863.[37] With the new year, much bigger battles were to come, again to test the mettle of the much-maligned Texas cavalrymen turned infantry.

One of the intriguing sidebars in the story of Stirling's Plantation was the capture of Lieutenant Colonel Guess, Dutch's former commanding officer in the 31st. Shortly before the battle, Guess had been placed under arrest by Colonel Speight on a charge of trading with the enemy. It was alleged that he had in his possession one million dollars in United States currency, with which he was to buy cotton for Federal speculators who slipped back and forth between the lines throughout the bayou country.[38]

It was well known that there were thousands of bales of cotton moldering on Louisiana plantations. The Confederate government had issued orders to burn all of it, since there was no way to transport it to a port where blockade runners would gladly test the Union navy's patrols. Plenty of Confederates, however, were willing to sell cotton for gold or U.S. greenbacks to the horde of traders who ubiquitously hovered around the Yankee army. Some Confederates justified selling to the enemy on the grounds that, with hard currency, they could buy supplies for their hard-pressed countrymen.[39] Others sold cotton for more mercenary reasons.

Guess, however, claimed that the charges were an "infernal, diabolical, damned lie" which was levied against him by Colonel Speight for personal reasons.[40] Although under arrest at the time, Guess accompanied his regiment into the Stirling Plantation battle. Following the battle on September 29, Guess was roaming the blood-soaked field of combat, ostensibly tending to some of the previously undiscovered wounded who were still lying in agony along the Morganza road, when he was surprised by a Union cavalry patrol and taken prisoner.[41]

It was a most peculiar capture, since a truce had been arranged between the Union and Confederate commanders that lasted from late September 29 through October 1, for the express purpose of allowing both sides to bring in the wounded, who were strewn all the way from the plantations' cane fields to the bayous extending along the Morganza road.[42] Under the circumstances, one might conjure up a picture of Lieutenant Colonel Guess frantically galloping after the retreating Yankee cavalry, shouting, "I surrender! I surrender!" For Guess, it may have been a fortuitous capture, since eating well in the officer's mess of a Yankee prison camp may have had certain advantages over a Confederate court-martial board whose sentences sometimes were less than lenient.

After returning to their camp at Morgan's Ferry, Dutch and the

Texans recuperated for several days until October 5, when they were ordered to march westward to Moundville. With Colonel Hawpe virtually a deserter and Lieutenant Colonel Guess a prisoner who faced a court martial if he ever were exchanged, Dutch and the 31st came under the command of the Mexican War veteran, Maj. Frederick J. Malone.[43]

Blessedly, the rain stopped, and the brigade stepped off in high spirits. For the next two weeks, they marched and countermarched in response to Yankee invasion rumors. The monotony of camp and march was broken on October 13, when Colonel Speight, health seemingly restored, rejoined the brigade after a sojourn in Texas. But, on October 18, the Texans went into angry shock when the command of the brigade was transferred to another officer.

Brig. Gen. Camille Armand Jules Marie, Prince de Polignac, stood before his ragged Texans. His keen dark eyes swept over the remaining seven hundred large, shambling men. His pearly white teeth gleamed brilliantly, as, with a large smile, he gave a twirl to his black, waxed mustache and then stroked his trim Napoleonic beard. His short, slight frame seemed to ooze satisfaction. They would do, he thought.

His broad smile was not reciprocated. "By God, this is too much," the Texans growled. Being sick, hungry, ragged, and wet; being thrown into battle without sleep against hordes of soldiers who massively outgunned them—if all that wasn't enough, now they would be commanded by "a damn frog eating Frenchman" with an unpronounceable name.[44] They exhibited more than disgust; their response bordered on mutiny. Dutch and the rest of his buddies found an approximate pronunciation for the proud royal name. Holding their noses, they ambled around "searching for General Polecat." This, however, was too much even for Texas troops, and General Taylor intervened.

The petite thirty-one-year-old Frenchman, Taylor said, was a professional soldier who had fought with distinction in the bloody trenches at Sevastopol during the Crimean War, waged by France and her allies against Russia. At the outbreak of the American Civil

Prince Camille de Polignac, who led the Texans on a wild charge at the battle of Mansfield. Courtesy Institute of Texan Cultures, University of Texas, San Antonio, Texas

War, he had left France and joined the Confederate army as a lieutenant colonel of infantry. Shortly afterward, he had been made chief of staff to Gen. Pierre T. G. Beauregard, the Confederate hero of First Manassas.

At a battle at Richmond, Kentucky, in August, 1862, Polignac had seized the fallen colors of the 5th Tennessee Infantry Regiment, "bearing them triumphantly through the thickest of the fight and encouraged the men to withstand a terrible fire."[45] Rapidly promoted to colonel and then to brigadier general, Polignac was more than a fashion plate destined only to strut among his Texas ragamuffins. The man could fight. Taylor later wrote: "I assembled the officers, and pointed out the consequences of disobedience, for which I should hold them accountable; but promised that if they remained dissatisfied with their new commander after an action, I would then remove him."[46]

Since the "consequences of disobedience" of any order given by General Taylor could mean a last look down six rifle barrels while the drums played the death march, the Texans settled down to murmured grumbling about the natty Frenchman, who discreetly decided not to hear. When the time came, Polignac knew that he would show his surly troops how a French nobleman behaved under fire.

The air cleared slightly when Colonel Speight, who never had quite recovered his health, again became ill and was forced to give up his command and return to Texas. A consolidated brigade then was formed under Polignac, consisting of the 15th Texas Infantry, the 22nd Dismounted Cavalry, the 31st Dismounted Cavalry, the 34th Dismounted Cavalry, the 17th Texas Consolidated Dismounted Cavalry, and the 11th Texas Battalion.[47]

Colonel Harrison, in a frank conversation with the Frenchman, outlined the problems of the brigade. Standards were not being enforced by the officers, he said; there was a lack of discipline, as well as ragged clothing, rotten shoes, chronic sickness, poor rations, and a shortage or even absence of medical supplies.[48]

Polignac could neither provide clothing and medical supplies nor improve the men's diet, but he did set standards for the officers and improve the sloppiness of the drill. After a few weeks, Dutch, in his rotting homespuns, might not have passed for a member of Napoleon's Imperial Guard, but at least he could march in step and do a respectable manual of arms. Most important, he could still fight like hell.

The paucity of proper uniforms almost caused a tragedy one day in October, when a column of blue-clad infantry was spotted a short distance from camp. As the alarm went out and troops rushed to an improvised firing line, anxiety turned to laughter when the approaching troops turned out to be not "Yankee blue bellies" but soldiers of General Mouton's Louisiana Division, who, after capturing Federal supply wagons, threw away their gray and butternut rags and put on brand-new jackets of Union blue.[49]

On another occasion, confusion over uniforms did lead to tragedy. Union Maj. Gen. Cadwallader C. Washburn reported that a captain of the 24th Iowa Infantry, while out on a foraging party near Opelousas, saw a group of men about half a mile away dressed in blue uniforms. Assuming that they were Federal troops, the captain rode up to them. As he approached the blue-clad soldiers, they gave a snappy salute, acknowledged by the officer. When he got closer, one of them shot him through the heart. Washburn reported, "They robbed him of his clothing, watch and pistol, and fled."[50]

As the drill of Dutch's brigade continued, the Texans began to perceive what they considered to be splendid character traits in their new commander. Not averse to wagering on everything from horse races to lice fights, the little Frenchman, after a bacchanalian night with whatever strong drink was available, was likely to burst forth with endless choruses of "Madam Gregoire," a bawdy French song extolling the virtues of a Parisian "lady of the evening."[51]

By October 26, one of Dutch's buddies in Company "C," Pvt. D. D. Whetston, noted, "General Polignac is quite a gentleman and is very well liked."[52] The bonds of admiration and affection between the minuscule general and his big lumbering Texans would only grow stronger in the coming months. By the end of October, the Texans again took up the march, hiking fruitlessly to and fro in response to Federal movements, as a pleasant autumn turned into an unusually cold winter.[53]

Late November found the Texans camping along the west bank of the Mississippi River, near Hogs Point. It was a dull business of standing picket duty in ever-drizzling rain, occasionally sniping inconclusively at Union gunboats running up and down the river, and, because of the usual lack of food, dreaming of hot, cooked meals and home.[54]

On December 3, the brigade was moved again. Marching by the old battlefield of Stirling's Plantation on Bayou Fordoche, Dutch saw that the interminable rain had washed away the shallow graves of some of the regiment's fallen, exposing the grotesque, bloated, blackened, and rotting bodies of dead friends. A burial detail hastily was assigned to the horrid job of reburying its dead comrades.[55] The men marched on, passing through the swamp country and coming out into a high, rolling prairie interspersed with densely forested areas.

By mid-December, the peripatetic Texans were hiking through piney woods country near Monroe. The area was thinly settled and inhabited by unusually poor farmers. The brigade spent Christmas in the woods on short rations, as usual. On December 29, Dutch's regiment, along with the rest of Polignac's Brigade, crossed the Red River and took up a position along a levee bordering the Black River, where they opened fire on a flock of Yankee gunboats heading upriver. One soldier reported, "General Polignac's troops fought them an entire day from behind the levee, killing many of their pilots and gunners."[56]

New Years Eve found the 31st camped three miles below Monroe, about eighty miles west of Vicksburg on the Bayou D'Arbonne. Private Whetston perhaps summed up the feelings of the whole brigade, as the new year dawned, when he wrote: "It was freezing all day. I have been in the war now nearly two years and I am afraid that it will be some time yet before it will come to a close. I hope that the end is near. I have seen enough to satisfy me."[57]

Capt. George W. O'Brien of the 11th Battalion of Texas Volunteers phrased it this way: "It is certainly very aggravating after marching so hard . . . to lie up and dream of the postponed happiness of arriving home. . . . I will go to sleep and try to quit thinking, to dream of home."[58]

During a few weeks of comparative calm, Dutch and his fellow

Texans suffered the usual shortages of rations and blankets. On long winter nights, the men cut logs and built roaring fires. After the ground had warmed, they shifted the logs aside and hunkered down on the warm ground while taking turns feeding the fire.[59]

Life was not entirely grim, however, and one of the troopers from Walker's Division recounted how the men huddled around campfires "singing, joking and laughing." Near one fire, he said, fiddlers were playing a merry tune, while some of the soldiers "were dancing jigs, reels and doubles," while others slapped their knees in time to the music.[60] Without proper clothing, dancing was, of course, one way to keep warm.

Some of the men held evening prayer meetings and sang old hymns they had learned at their mothers' knees. A few just stared into the darkness, wondering if the future held for them the death of a badly wounded soldier, lingering for days, "tortured by thirst and pain, his festering wounds creeping with maggots, his tongue swollen, and a fierce fever festering upon his body."[61]

During January, "jayhawking" depredations were causing many of the contested areas of Louisiana to revert to barbarism. Jayhawkers, as they commonly were called, were deserters from both the Confederate and Union armies, who hid out in the swamps and woods and raided isolated farms, stealing anything valuable and raping and killing any helpless inhabitants upon whom they could lay their bestial hands. The jayhawkers were rightly regarded by both armies as the scum of the earth. Not only did they offer a refuge for draft dodgers, but also they impeded recruitment, because many men refused to be inducted into the army for fear of leaving their families to the mercy of these human hyenas. On several occasions, General Taylor ordered the 31st to scour jayhawker-infested areas. If caught, he ordered, they were not to be arrested, but troopers were to shoot "every man found with arms in his hands."[62]

The 31st also was ordered to round up conscripts and to sweep the countryside for horses and mules that might fall into the hands of advancing Federals. Dutch and his fellow Texans pursued this job with an overabundance of enthusiasm and managed to denude the countryside of everything on four legs, leading Private Whetston to complain, "Our command pressed . . . mules from the citizens which I think is not a very good plan. . . . a bad policy."[63]

Confederate headquarters in Shreveport didn't think it was a good plan either—not after outraged farm owners complained loudly and angrily to General Taylor. Polignac was ordered to return many of the mules and horses and was reminded that he was to take only animals that might fall into Yankee hands, not to round up every beast in Louisiana.[64] Reluctantly, Dutch and his friends turned back their newly assembled *remudas*—at least the parts they didn't eat.

In late January, tired of chasing jayhawkers and rounding up stray mules, Polignac suggested to General Taylor that he launch a raid behind the Federal lines, at Vidalia on the west bank of the Mississippi River. In early February, Taylor approved the plan. Polignac took two regiments of cavalry, Dutch and the 31st, one other infantry regiment, and six pieces of artillery, and on Sunday morning, February 7, slipped out of camp headed for the unsuspecting Yankee forces near Vidalia.[65] The troops were hungry; one of them had written, "Our beef is poor as a snake." They marched off with alacrity, however; after all, they might capture some good Yankee rations during the raid.[66]

By four o'clock in the afternoon, after a forced march, the mixed force of eight hundred Texans surprised the Yankee garrison at Vidalia, attacking through hazy winter light. The Federals responded with a few artillery shells and then ordered a general retreat, falling back to their gunboats. With steam whistles blowing wildly and frenzied cries of "Cast off," the entire Federal fleet steamed off down the river. After burying the lone Texan killed by the fire of the gunboats and making their three wounded men as comfortable as possible, the men rounded up some four hundred horses, mules, and cattle in the Union camp area.[67]

Most welcome was a large supply of rations stored at Vidalia. Not only had this been an easy battle, but Dutch and his fellow troopers, gloating over the Yankee food, were able, in a rare moment, to eat their fill.[68] Then the infantry fanned out and rounded up a large number of slaves, who were returned to Harrisonburg to work on fortifications the Confederates were building there to protect the town from gunboat attacks.

The cavalry rode off to raid and "break up" a number of plantations in the Lake Concordia region. These had been seized by groups loyal to the Union, for the purpose of producing cotton for the Federal government. This—"preventing the colonization of our lands by foreign abolitionists"—was the most important aspect of Polignac's daring raid, according to Confederate headquarters.[69]

Loaded with loot, Polignac's men fell back to Harrisonburg. The captured slaves were sent to the small town of Trinity on the Black River, where they began to muscle three heavy 32-pounder artillery pieces onto the mud-and-log breastworks being erected there. The brigade rested at Harrisonburg until, on March 1, a Yankee fleet consisting of the gunboats *Ouachita*, *Fort Hindman*, *Osage*, *Lexington*, *Conestoga*, and *Cricket* sailed up the Black River and began to pound the incomplete fortifications at Trinity.

To fight on the western rivers, boats had to have flat bottoms and shallow drafts. Since there was no need for seaworthiness on the relatively smooth river waters, the boats could be much wider, in proportion to their lengths, than seagoing ships. Also, unlike bluewater vessels, usually they did not attack broadside on, but rather shot from the wide, heavily armed bow, which sometimes contained as many as four big guns.

Gunboats were propelled by paddle wheels. These wheels were driven by a reciprocating steam engine which burned wood or coal in its boilers and produced a long plume of smoke through tall smokestacks providing a natural draft.[70]

Weaponry consisted of muzzle-loading cannon which fired either solid shot, used against fortifications; and explosive shot, or canister, used against personnel. Among the gunboats standing off Harrisonburg, the *Conestoga* and the *Lexington* were wooden-hulled former freight and passenger steamers that had been converted into warships. Each was 180 feet long and 42 feet wide, with a displacement of 535 tons and a six-foot draft. Each boat was driven by two sidewheel steam engines.

The *Lexington* was armed with two guns, each weighing more than two tons and throwing 32-pound shells; and four eight-inch guns, each weighing more than three tons. The *Conestoga* was armed with four 32-pounders. Both boats were protected by oak bulwarks five inches thick, which could stop infantry musket balls but not artillery shells.[71]

The *Osage* was a stern-wheel monitor, with a low, raftlike deck mounting two 11-inch cannons in a cylindrical armored turret. The big guns fired massive 121-pound shells. More important, this heavy hitter could operate in less than four feet of water.[72]

The *Fort Hindman* was a typical "tinclad," with two big guns mounted in the bow. "Tinclads" were protected by quarter-inch plates of iron, which gave protection mainly against rifle fire. The *Cricket*, a "tinclad" similar to the *Fort Hindman*, served as Rear Adm. David Dixon Porter's flagship.

The boats could make no more than five to eight knots, slower than a galloping horse, but their ability to fight in shallow water at close ranges with tremendous hitting power made them formidable adversaries, as Dutch and his friends soon would discover.[73]

At Trinity, the Confederate artillerymen had only one of the big guns mounted and ready to fire. There was, however, one other problem. The quartermasters had failed to deliver the proper ammunition for the guns. Chagrined, Polignac reluctantly ordered the three big cannons dumped into the river. While his light 12-pounders blazed away at the fleet chugging down the stream, Dutch and the rest of the infantry ran along the river bank like madmen, occasionally throwing themselves down on the levee to draw a bead and snipe at any exposed sailors. Undeterred, the Union fleet shelled the Trinity position into rubble and then turned downriver to Harrisonburg, chased by the running and firing Texans who followed the boats along the riverbank as daylight faded.[74]

That night the Union fleet anchored out in the river, but at ten o'clock the next morning, the ships appeared off Harrisonburg to renew the battle. Dutch and the rest of the infantry were waiting along the banks of the Black River. Polignac's artillery, however, had been reduced to only a section of 6-pounder Parrot guns. The other artillery pieces had been rendered useless by broken caissons or horses exhausted during the wild race down the river the previous evening.[75]

As the Yankee fleet and the Texas troops opened up on one another, the battle was somewhat less than equal. As Polignac ruefully reported, "The iron clads were safe against my artillery, and the wooden boats were protected from the musketry by a plate of sheet iron between two thicknesses of wood on their sides."[76]

Moving closer, the fleet riddled houses in the town with incendiary shot, causing some of them to burst into flames. Dutch and the other infantrymen were called into service as firemen and, after "considerable exertion," smothered the flames, saving most of the town. At dusk the fleet withdrew back up the river. Polignac reported, "The enemy fired not less than 1,000 rounds, out of 24- and 32-pounders and 12-pound Parrot guns and guns of smaller caliber, a great deal of grape, canisters and spherical case and some 8- and 11-inch shells. . . .The troops on board fired through loopholes." The result of this massive display of Federal firepower was a Confederate loss of six men killed and ten wounded.[77]

All things considered, the Texans had not done badly. Union Rear Adm. David D. Porter reported that "*Fort Hindman* was badly cut up with shot and shell," the *Osage* had become disabled when the main wheel of the turret was smashed, the *Ouachita* had suffered one sailor killed and two wounded. Overall, the fleet had had two killed and fourteen wounded by the outmanned Texans. Before withdrawing, however, the naval forces burned a pontoon bridge over a nearby river, picked up an unknown number of cotton bales, and retrieved from the river the three big guns that Polignac had dumped there.[78]

While Admiral Porter termed the operation "perfectly successful," General Taylor also claimed victory, writing, "The gunboats were driven off and Polignac by his coolness under fire, gained the confidence of his men, as he soon gained their affections by his care and attention."[79] This bonding of the Texans with their tough little French leader was vital, as soon their loyalty and courage were to be tested in the biggest and most savage series of battles ever to rock the battered state of Louisiana.

CHAPTER 8

The Red River Campaign

While Dutch and his comrades were marching and countermarching through the prostrate parishes of southern Louisiana, far away in Washington, D.C., pressures were building which would result in the bloodiest battles ever fought in the Trans-Mississippi West.

Ever since the beginning of the war, Union strategists had been pondering ways to strip Texas from the Confederacy. The greatest impetus for the invasion of Texas, more important than either military or political considerations, was pressure from textile mill owners of the Northeast. With their mills almost totally idle since the war's inception, they not only had suffered serious financial losses, but also they feared that rival English manufacturers would be supplied with southern cotton, courtesy of blockade runners. Having heard rumors that thousands of bales of cotton were lying in warehouses north and west of the Union lines outside of New Orleans and along the borders of Texas, they pushed Lincoln for military action which would enable them to seize these vast bonanzas.

A secondary reason for the North to invade the Lone Star State had to do with the political situation in Mexico. In late 1861, French,

British, and Spanish troops invaded that country, to force its government to pay debts owed to European merchants. By June, 1863, the British and Spanish had left, but French troops had occupied Mexico City and driven President Benito Juárez from the country. Napoleon III of France was planning to place an Austrian Hapsburg on the throne of Mexico and make that country part of an expanding French empire.

On August 5, President Lincoln wrote to General Banks, "Recent events in Mexico, I think, render early action in Texas more important than ever." It was necessary, according to Lincoln, to show the flag in Texas to deter the French.[1] If the principle was to uphold the Monroe Doctrine, the practical reason was to prevent the French from giving any aid to the Confederacy.

After two amphibious expeditions, one at Galveston and the other at Sabine Pass, had failed, Gen. Henry Halleck, the Union chief of staff, urged that Texas be invaded by troops advancing up the Red River to Shreveport and then driving westward into the Lone Star State.

At first, Banks was dubious. A former governor of Massachusetts and Speaker of the U.S. House of Representatives, he was untrained in military tactics and had obtained his major general's rank through political influence. During Stonewall Jackson's campaign in the Shenandoah Valley in 1862, Banks had been totally outgeneraled and thoroughly trounced time and again by inferior Rebel forces. Indeed, Banks had lost so many military and commissary supplies to the fast-moving Jackson that he was contemptuously called the Confederacy's best supply officer.

Massive reinforcements and, probably, pressure from his old constituents, the Massachusetts cotton mill owners, soon changed Banks's mind. With ten thousand veteran troops borrowed from Gen. William T. Sherman's tough army, his own force of twenty-five thousand troops, and a fleet of fourteen ironclads, six tinclads, and approximately forty supply vessels, mounting more than two hundred heavy cannon, Banks was ready to move. To put further pressure on the small Confederate army in Louisiana, a Union force of fifteen thousand troops stationed in Arkansas was to attack southward, trapping the Rebels in a giant pincer movement.

Banks, now in a chipper mood, dressed the part of the dashing soldier. He was, at forty-eight years of age, in the prime of life. He sported neat mustachios, an imperial beard, and boots polished to a shine in which admirers could see their reflection. Spotless buckskin gauntlets and a wide-brimmed hat set at a jaunty angle gave him the look of a latter-day D'Artagnan. In appearance, previous defeats had not dented his martial determination.[2]

On April 2, 1864, he bragged, writing to General Halleck in Washington, "We hope to be in Shreveport by the tenth of April. I do not fear concentration of the enemy at that point. My fear is that they may not be willing to meet us."[3] He need not have worried. President Lincoln, who had experience with the braggadocio of inept commanders, shrugged when he read Banks's message, remarking, "The next news we shall hear from there will be of a defeat."[4]

Facing this federal juggernaut was Gen. Richard Taylor, who, while soldiering with Stonewall Jackson, had learned to hold Banks in contempt. To oppose the invasion, Taylor had Maj. Gen. John G. Walker's hard-fighting Texas infantry division, a division of Louisiana and Texas troops that included the ragged but willing brigade of Texans commanded by Polignac, a few companies of Louisiana cavalry, and hard-riding Texas cavalry under Gen. Thomas Green.[5]

By mid-March, the federal army began moving up the Red River by both a road paralleling the river and on the waterway. On March 12, their combined operations had taken Simmesport; the Confederate entrenchments at Fort de Russy were quickly captured. By March 15, the fleet was in Alexandria. The hard-pressed Confederates continued retreating northward.

When the Federal fleet confronted low water and rapids near Alexandria, Adm. David Porter, who had boasted that his gunboats could go "anywhere the sand is damp," delayed until the Red River rose with spring flooding. Finally he crossed the rapids with twelve gunboats and about thirty supply ships, although one steamer was wrecked in the process.[6]

While part of the Union force hiked along the narrow, dusty river road, the luckier ones took their leisure, loafing on the decks of the supply vessels as they steamed on north to Natchitoches, reaching that river port on April 3. From there they made a short march to Grand Ecore. It was at the latter place that Banks made a decision that was to determine the fate of the invasion.

Although he was less than 150 miles south of Shreveport, his first major objective, Banks was being pressured by General Sherman to hurry his campaign and return the borrowed ten thousand veterans. In order to save time, Banks determined to abandon the river road and follow a stagecoach road, the Old Stage Road, that ran from Grand Ecore westward to the little town of Many and then north to Shreveport, passing through the towns of Pleasant Hill and Mansfield. He planned to rendezvous at Loggy Bayou a hundred miles to the north, where the river and the road met, at a point only thirty miles south of Shreveport. There were, however, drawbacks. For more than one hundred miles, the Yankee column would be stretched out along a narrow country road, heavily forested on both sides, and the force would be without a major source of water.

During that long, hot march, the Federal army would not have the two hundred heavy cannon of Porter's fleet to provide overwhelming artillery support against any Confederate forces which tried to impede its advance.

Admiral Porter may have been happy to see Banks depart. It freed him to roam the rivers searching for cotton to seize. Unlike the army, which turned confiscated bales over to the government without compensation, the U.S. Navy was in business for itself. Following the old high seas tradition of prize money, when the navy impounded cotton—belonging, they of course claimed, to the Confederate government—they sold it on the open market, and the captain and crew of the ship that captured it split the profits.

It was reported that, when a trove of the precious fiber was located near a river town, Porter's gunboats would debouch on the place, menacing it with their big guns, while a landing party, ostensibly to conform with the law, stenciled "C.S.A." on each captured cotton bale. An irate army colonel remarked that the letters really meant "Cotton Stealing Association of the U.S. Navy" and it became a mordant joke on the New Orleans waterfront. When Admiral Porter heard it, it was said, he laughed as loudly as anyone else.[7] The joke was considered less than funny by the blue-clad men who were soon to spill their blood for the profit of sailors and the horde of cotton speculators who hung around them like vultures around carrion.

On April 6, Banks's army, slowed down by more than a thousand cumbersome supply wagons, waved a cheery farewell to the fleet and set off down the hilly country road. At the small town of Mansfield, a tough little army of southerners waited. It was, for them, after a two-hundred-mile retreat, a time of high tension.

Private Blessington of Walker's Division recounted how, one night, a nervous sentry fired his musket into the darkness after he heard a "heavy tramp," which, he believed, signaled an attack by Yankee cavalry. "The troops all of a sudden stampeded, some of them running down the bank of a creek . . . while others jumped a fence on the left of the road." To add to the confusion, some jester shouted, "Charge against cavalry!" As nervous troops fixed bayonets and cocked muskets, from out of the darkness tramped, not Yankee cavalry but two bewildered steers that had wandered onto the road.[8]

But nightly jitters gave way to daylight determination as, outnumbered and outgunned as usual, the Texas troops, "with compressed lips and blanched faces," moved into Mansfield to the tune of "Dixie," while the town's ladies "threw their bright garlands at the feet of the brave Texas boys, beseeching them in God's name to drive back the enemy." "We felt," Blessington said, "that although greatly outnumbered [we] would in the end be victorious."[9]

By late afternoon on April 7, Tom Green's Texas cavalry had skirmished with the Federal advance guard near Pleasant Hill, while, a few miles to the north, outside the little town of Mansfield, General Taylor studied the ground to his front and made his dispositions. He had retreated far enough. Here he would stand and fight.

The bloody battle at Pleasant Hill in April, 1864, where Union generals snatched defeat from the jaws of victory. Courtesy Institute of Texan Cultures, University of Texas, San Antonio, Texas

On the morning of April 8, the Confederate line of battle was formed up across the Old Stage Road three miles south of Mansfield and one mile east of Sabine Crossroads, where four country roads forked. Sheltered in forest and brush but facing a cleared area some twelve hundred yards deep by eight hundred yards wide, they would not easily be visible to troops marching down the road. On the right flank were Texas cavalry and Walker's Texas infantry. To the left of the road, a Texas infantry brigade was posted; aligned next to them was General Mouton's mixed division of Texas and Louisiana troops, which included Polignac's Texans. Shoulder to shoulder were the 22nd Dismounted Cavalry, Dutch's 31st Dismounted Cavalry, 34th Dismounted Cavalry, 15th Infantry, and the 17th Dismounted Cavalry.

That day—after months of lousy food, inadequate shelter, sickness without medical supplies, and tattered clothes rotting on their backs; with obsolete or captured arms—they stood there. Perhaps Dutch and his comrades remembered the biting words of generals who had cursed their sloppy frontier discipline, their sometimes stumbling drill, and their insolent, mocking manner.

That day, they would face a magnificently drilled and equipped army, fed on nourishing food, with the best uniforms an industrial nation could supply, with wagons full of medical supplies. The Federals' weapons were the most modern in the world, and they had endless supplies of ammunition. Least important to the Confederates and their leaders, the southerners would be outnumbered at least three to one.

That day, those Texans stood under the hot Louisiana sun, facing a wide open clearing—and waited. They were ready. As Capt. Elijah Petty of Walker's Division wrote home, "The earth will shake and the wool fly."[10]

That morning, General Taylor rode along his lines, viewing his troops with an appraising eye. Riding up to Polignac, who was sitting astride his charger, Taylor pulled up on his reins and shouted, "Little Frenchman, I am going to fight Banks here if he has a million men."[11]

Banks, too, was confident. That morning he entrusted his line of march to Gen. William B. Franklin, whom he considered an experienced and competent officer. Franklin, only a few weeks previously, had bungled a seaborne invasion off Sabine Pass, Texas, allowing a Houston saloon keeper and two score of his customers, in a mud fort with only five big guns, to cripple and drive off a Federal fleet accompanied by a division of veteran troops.

Early that morning of April 8, the Federal army began marching down the narrow Old Stage Road, flanked by trees and underbrush. General Taylor later wrote, "Five thousand mounted men led the advance, followed by a long wagon train and much artillery. Infantry succeeded, then more wagons and artillery, then infantry again . . . the front and rear of his column were separated by a distance of 20 miles."[12] It was a tactical disposition that was to prove decisive.

Stating that Banks had twenty-five thousand troops, Taylor wrote, "I had on the field fifty-three hundred infantry, three thousand horse and five hundred artillerymen—in all, eight thousand, eight hundred men."[13]

Advance units of Federal and Confederate cavalry skirmished all morning and through the early afternoon, as the Union main body slowly approached the Rebel positions. By four o'clock that afternoon, ever-impatient Taylor, seeing Union cavalry dismounting and forming skirmisher lines, as well as infantry and artillery deploying to his front, rode up to Brig. Gen. Alfred Mouton, who was commanding the bulk of Taylor's troops on the left flank, and gave the order to attack.

Mouton, thirty-five years old, was described as "a noble-looking man, of fine, dignified appearance. He was a courteous, refined gentleman and a brave officer."[14] After receiving his orders, Mouton rode to Polignac's side and said, "Let us charge them right in the face and throw them into the valley." With this he drew his saber and rode to the front of his division.[15]

Polignac galloped to the front of his men and drew his sword. Sweeping off his black-plumed hat and placing it on the end of his long blade, he thrust his arm aloft and shouted, "My Texans, follow yer ol' polecat."[16] Screaming their shrill battle cry, Dutch and the Texans burst out of the woods, running at full speed at the Union formations. Private Blessington, at the other end of the Rebel line, found that "shells, canister, and bullets are falling around like a hail storm," as brigade commanders rode along the line of their advancing troops shouting encouragement. "There was no faltering, but wild cheers. . . . Onward our troops advance[d], pale with excitement, compressed lips and blazing eyes," while the battered flags of the charging regiments were thrust forward in defiance of the enemy fire.[17]

Taylor watched the battle, calmly sitting on his horse, one leg languidly thrust over the pommel of his saddle, smoking a cigar. Not a man who gave accolades freely, he later reported of Dutch and the much-maligned dismounted cavalry regiments, "The charge made by Mouton across the open was magnificent. With his little division, consisting of his own and Polignac's brigades, the field was crossed under a murderous fire of artillery and musketry. Despite . . . heavy losses of officers and men, the division never halted."[18]

Two hundred yards from a rail fence, held in force by the Union troops, Dutch and the 31st reeled from a "storm of rifle fire and grapeshot." But Mouton, laughing and cheering, waved them forward; as Polignac, churning his sword with the feathered hat high overhead, screamed, "Come on boys, come on!" Rallying, the Texans charged again. As they reached the fence, the Federals broke and fell back, and Dutch and his inflamed comrades scrambled over the wooden rails. Mouton, however, fell with a half-dozen missiles piercing his body. With Mouton dead, Polignac took command of the division, driving it forward into the broken Union lines.[19]

Walker's Division on the right flank also was attacking viciously, and the Union line crumbled into a mass of running, beaten men. And this was where General Franklin's blundering line of march caused defeat to turn into a rout. Banks was unable to bring up infantry or artillery reinforcements quickly, because men and guns had to wend their way past hundreds of supply wagons stalled along the narrow Old Stage Road. Surrounding forest and underbrush also prevented the wagons from turning around.

While they were outnumbered almost three to one, the Confederates, due to Union confusion, had a numerical superiority at the firing line. The impetus of their headlong attack drove the fleeing Federal infantry back onto their transport wagons, causing the teamsters to flee in panic, abandoning tons of precious supplies. Unable to maneuver, the muscle-bound Union army saw its head driven back into its mid-section and tail.

Banks, if he lacked brains, had no shortage of guts; and he rode up and down among the fleeing troops, trying to rally the panicked men into a defensive line. Cavalrymen without horses, artillerymen without cannon, infantrymen who had thrown away their rifles, and teamsters who had abandoned their wagons streamed down the road in an undisciplined mass. An eastern war correspondent wrote that he was "swallowed up . . . in a hissing, seething, bubbling whirlpool of agitated men."[20] These men were hotly pursued by the Texans, shrieking their terrible half-Comanche and half-Mexican cry, a cacophony well designed to urge on frightened men.

The broken Yankees streamed past a new battle line formed by the fresh troops of Brig. Gen. William Emory's 1st Division of the Federal XIX Corps. Emory formed a line of battle along a wooded hill named Pleasant Grove. In the waning hours of the afternoon, Dutch's 31st and other units attacked Federal units at a small creek close to the grove, where they paused to gulp large draughts of water into gunpowder-parched throats. Taylor later wrote, "Possession of the water was all-important, for there was none other between this [place] and Mansfield. Walker, Green, and Polignac led on their weary men, and I rode down to the stream. There was some sharp work but we persisted, the enemy fell back and the stream was held."[21]

The Battle of Mansfield was the high-water mark of Banks's invasion. Never again would the Union armies attempt to sever Texas from the Confederacy. Dutch and the rest of the slandered ragamuffins of Polignac's dismounted cavalry had fought their hearts out, and never again would their valor or fitness for combat be questioned.

Taylor's little army had inflicted more than twenty-two hundred casualties upon the Union intruders. They had captured twenty artillery pieces, hundreds of small arms, more than a thousand horses and mules, and, most important of all, more than two hundred wagons fully loaded with all sorts of badly needed military supplies. For the first time in months, Dutch was able to indulge in a meal of good bacon, edible bread, and real coffee. Again, Gen. Nathaniel Banks had proved to be the best commissary officer in the Confederate army.

The battle was won, however, at heavy cost to Dutch and his comrades. The less than 2,200 men in Polignac's Brigade suffered 762 casualties, more than one-third of their number. Polignac was among those slightly wounded.[22]

That night Banks decided to fall back fourteen miles to Pleasant Hill, where he could stabilize a defensive line with fresh troops who had been unable to reach the Mansfield battlefield. Taylor also received reinforcements and planned an attack the next day. Walker's and Polignac's exhausted men would be kept in reserve.

As the Confederate troops marched toward Pleasant Hill on the morning of April 9, a touch of macabre humor rippled down their lines. A long file of downcast-looking soldiers being led to the rear received ribald hoots and hollers from the Johnny Rebs. They were captured Zouaves, probably those of the 165th New York Infantry. With their ballooning, bloomerlike, red Turkish pants, they were confused, the Rebels claimed, with women in skirts. "We've whipped all the men and now we have to whip their women," they hooted. Some of the Texans laid down their muskets, saying, with mock gallantry, that they refused to shoot at girls in bloomers.[23]

Tired but still full of fight, the Rebel forces tramped along the Old Stage Road to Pleasant Hill, passing the remains of burned wagons, dead mules, disgorged packs, and bloating corpses. Shortly after noon, they came upon the Union army, drawn up across a high ridge on the left of the road and extending to a wooded hill on the right. In front was a ditch cut by winter water runoff that was held by skirmishers. The main body of the Federal forces was spread out on high ground to their rear.

Hot and thirsty after the fourteen-mile march, the Confederates rested during the midday hours. Undoubtedly thoughts turned to home, as well as to the coming battle. Veterans now, the Texans were determined, if fatalistic. Perhaps typical was Capt. Elijah Petty, who, sometime earlier, had written to his small son: "I am afraid an invasion . . . is intended. . . . But my son before they get to you all they will leave many a bloody track behind them. . . . for we must and will contest every inch of ground. . . . Be a good boy. You may not have a father to advise you and support and protect you long and you may have to rely upon yourself. . . . Remember me kindly."[24]

About four o'clock in the afternoon, Taylor ordered the attack. Dutch and the 31st, with the rest of Polignac's battered brigade, were in reserve on the left flank of the charging Rebel line. But Pleasant Hill was not another Mansfield, and Confederate attacks, although partly successful, at first were driven back with heavy losses. Soon Walker and Polignac's troops were rushed forward to back up the faltering Confederate ranks.

Again, although wounded, Polignac rode before his men with his hat on the end of his sword and cried, "Texans, follow your Polignac." They did indeed follow their courageous little leader, but they were repulsed with heavy losses.[25] General Walker was carried from the field after being shot in the groin, while the prescient Capt. Elijah Petty was shot through the chest with grapeshot and fell dead leading his men.[26] As he had feared, his little son would have to grow up without a father to protect and advise him.

As night fell, Taylor broke off the futile attacks and withdrew six miles, to a place where there was a stream with running water. All that night, both Billy Yank and Johnny Reb conducted an unofficial truce as they roamed the battlefield in search of wounded comrades crying for water and moaning in agony. A Federal surgeon saw "headless trunks, scattered limbs, and bodies torn into fragments." The next day hundreds of buzzards gorged on dead horses, while a multitude of green flies feasted on the bodies of American dead.[27]

If the battlefield that night recalled a scene from a surreal Hieronymus Bosch painting, the field hospitals were not much better. One soldier described a Confederate hospital as "resembling a butcher's shamble with maimed and bloody men lying . . . some with their arms off; some with their legs off . . . piles of bloody looking limbs are strewn around."[28]

If the valor of the Union defense had snatched victory from the jaws of defeat, that night the Union commanders snatched defeat from the jaws of their victory. While Banks sorely felt the loss of another fifteen hundred men during the day's battle, Taylor, with fewer men, had lost more than twelve hundred. Nevertheless, to the disgust of some of his subordinates, Banks and the equally inept Franklin, following a council of war, decided that they had had enough. Citing an inadequate supply of drinking water and the destruction of many of his supply wagons, Banks ordered a retreat back to Grand Ecore, where he could again shelter under the big guns of the Yankee fleet. In his hurry, he left behind some four hundred of his wounded men. By April 11, he was back at that river town, digging in and waiting for the fleet, which had gone upstream, to return.

Taylor, undismayed by his heavy losses at Pleasant Hill, wished to press his offensive and destroy Banks's entire army, but Gen. Kirby Smith, worried about the Federal troops advancing from Arkansas, withdrew the bulk of the little army and sent them north to check the Federal offensive from that direction. Taylor, in a rage, was left with only Green's cavalry and Polignac's shot-up infantry, totaling about five thousand men, to press the twenty-five thousand retreating Union troops. As Taylor's remaining men moved up to Grand Ecore, it became a rather strange siege, with the ragged Confederates bottling up five times their number.

On April 15, Porter's fleet arrived off Grand Ecore, after a bitterly contested trip downriver; his boats crashed into stumps and ran aground on mudbanks, as the water level of the river dropped. And while his boats were struggling, they were continually harassed by Tom Green's cavalry and a battery of four light field pieces, which shot at them continually. A Union soldier said that the sides of some of the transports were shot half away "and their smokestacks look like huge pepper boxes."[29] The gunboats replied by massively shelling the river banks with their big eleven-inch cannon, a tactic that was likened to "hunting partridges with a howitzer."[30]

Sadly for the Texans and luckily for the Union fleet, a blast of gunboat canister decapitated Gen. Tom Green, and the Texans broke off the battle.[31] But Porter, too, had had enough. With the Red River falling rapidly, he informed Banks that he was withdrawing downriver past the shallows and rapids at Alexandria. On April 21, the Union army and navy began a general retreat. Closely pressed by Polignac, the Yankee ground forces took time to burn Grand Ecore to the ground and then put the charming little town of Natchitoches to the torch.[32]

Just below Grand Ecore, one of the boats, the ironclad *Eastport*, hit a torpedo and became stranded. As other Federal boats came toward her to render aid, Polignac's ubiquitous dismounted cavalrymen peppered them with rifle fire, and Porter was forced to blow up the vessel to prevent its capture. Dutch and his fellows also managed to shoot up the gunboats *Juliet* and *Fort Hindman,* their old foes from the previous month's battle at Harrisonburg, leaving more than twenty casualties among the sailors. Porter's flagship, *Cricket*, came off even worse, when a Rebel battery inflicted thirty-one casualties on her crew of fifty.[33]

After days of skirmishing with Confederate cavalry and the hotly pursuing infantry, both the fleet and Banks's army reached Alexandria, where they were shut up for more than two weeks while Porter's boats, who could go "anywhere the sand was wet," struggled to get past the Red River shallows. After days of heroic labor and engineering genius, the Federal fleet managed, on May 13, to get over the falls at Alexandria. Again on parallel tracks, the fleet and the army retreated down the Red River.

"During the 14th, 15th and 16th," Dutch and the almost exhausted Texas infantry, according to Taylor, "constantly attacked in front, rear and right flank" of the retreating Union army.[34]

"We had a big fight," Dutch later recounted. "We had to march all night through swamps from ankle deep to waist deep to cut off the Yankees. . . . We got around them at daybreak and opened the battle at daylight before General Green's cavalry came up; the Yankees started to retreat and we had to run to a bend in the levee to stop them; the cavalry got past us but we got all of their artillery and a good many prisoners."[35]

Taylor admitted, however, "Our loss was heavy, four hundred and fifty two in killed and wounded; among the former, Colonel Stone, commanding Polignac's old brigade. Polignac, in charge of the division, was conspicuous in this action."[36] The battle, later called Yellow Bayou by the Confederates, was not a success. The Federal army inflicted heavy losses on the Confederates, with Polignac's troops again losing more than one-third of their remaining men. More importantly, the Federals managed to cross the Atchafalaya River close to its junction with the Mississippi, finally evading the clutches of Taylor's little army. Goliath successfully had eluded the wrath of little David.

After more than seventy days of uninterrupted fighting, the Red River expedition ended where it had begun—on the east bank of the Atchafalaya River. Ruefully, Taylor wrote, "In their rapid flight from Grand Ecore to Monette's Ferry, a distance of forty miles, the Federals burned nearly every house on the road. In pursuit, we passed the smoking ruins of homesteads, by which stood weeping women and children. Time for the removal of the most necessary articles of furniture had been refused. It was difficult to restrain one's inclinations to punish the ruffians engaged in this work, a number of whom were captured; but they asserted, and doubtless with truth, that they were acting under orders."[37]

The Union withdrawal marked the close of large-scale fighting between armed forces in the Trans-Mississippi Department; but in its aftermath, acrid recriminations and *ad hominem* attacks were leveled at many of the participants. An embittered General Taylor blamed Kirby Smith, who, he claimed, by recalling most of his troops northward, prevented Taylor from totally destroying Banks's army and capturing the stalled Union fleet. Had he been allowed to do so, he believed, he would have been able to recapture New Orleans, reopen the Mississippi, and reinforce the outnumbered Confederates in Georgia, enabling them to smash General Sherman's invading Federal army. In a flight related more to fancy than to reality, Taylor believed that he could have turned the tide of the war, ultimately achieving a triumph of the South. "The Southern people," he wrote, "might have been spared the humiliation of defeat, and the countless woes and wrongs inflicted on them by their conquerors."[38]

During the winter of 1864, General Polignac corresponded with friends in France and became convinced that, upon his return to Paris, he might be successful in gaining French aid and recognition for the Confederacy. Since it seemed doubtful that any further fighting was imminent in the Trans-Mississippi, he departed for France, crossing Texas, where he received a hero's welcome, and taking ship in Mexico.[39]

General Banks "experienced the ultimate humiliation of a commander when he was hissed by his troops."[40] His fiasco, the result of faulty tactics and a failure of nerve, had cost the lives of thousands of his soldiers. After his return to New Orleans, he never again was allowed to command troops in the field and virtually was reduced to the job of chief clerk in the Military Division of West Mississippi.[41]

For the weary Texans of Polignac's Brigade, there was little rest. They continued to harass Union forces until summer, when they were ordered to march to Arkansas in anticipation of a federal attack from there. Fortunately, they were involved in little fighting.

As for Dutch, after more than two years of hard campaigning; after dodging Minié balls and canister in hotly contested battles in Missouri, Arkansas, and Louisiana; after surviving starvation, exposure, and disease in those campaigns; his luck had run out. Following Yellow Bayou, he wrote: "After this fight I was taken sick and was sent to the hospital at Alexandria. While I was in the hospital I lost my sight."[42]

Dutch did not describe the conditions in the hospital at Alexandria, but his former regimental commander, Lieutenant Colonel Guess, earlier had written home to Texas, "There are about five doctors in our regiment and I am, this day, a better physician than any of them."[43]

Another soldier wrote, "There is more danger in a hospital than in the field of battle. I have never been in a hospital, but if I ever do have to go to one on account of sickness, I will make my will before starting."[44]

Dutch later wrote:

> When I got so I could see again I joined my command, but could not do duty so after a long time I was sent home. I had a hard time of it, as I was nearly blind, the trip was very hard on me to come from Louisiana to San Antonio.
>
> Some days I could not get a thing to eat and had to lie down in the woods. My eyes were so bad that I could not see a house fifty feet from the road. I was never asked for my pa-

> pers but once, that was between Beaumont and Jasper. Three men came to me and asked for my papers, I pointed to my eyes, but they wanted to know if I had any papers from my Commander, so I showed them my papers.
>
> They stayed with me a little while and got to talking [about] what we would do when we got our independence. They [said they] would run all the Dutch out of the country. I told them that they had better start now, as there was three to one, [and] that I was a Dutchman. They said, "We don't mean you."
>
> I got along the best I could until I got as far as Arlington, Texas. I was hungry and tired and was sitting beside the road when a boy spoke to me and called me by my name. I could not see him, [but] he told me he was Nat Hindes, one of my neighbor's boys. He took me with him and got me home alright.[45]

So, at the end of a footsore journey of more than three hundred miles, half-starved and blind, twenty-six-year-old Emil Frederick ("Dutch") Wurzbach staggered home to San Antonio, into the arms of his beloved Matilda. And there he would remain.

Epilogue

Charles Louis Wurzbach also survived the war. After the capitulation of the Confederacy, he was discharged as a captain and aide-de-camp to the Confederate general commanding at Galveston, Texas.

After returning to San Antonio, he volunteered again for a short foray with the Texas Rangers before marrying in 1866. He was admitted to the State Bar of Texas in 1870 and served as city attorney for San Antonio from 1872 until 1875, during which time he compiled and codified the ordinances of that city. Charles was elected to the state legislature as the Bexar County representative for the Fifteenth through the Eighteenth Texas Legislatures. Then he served three terms as county judge of Bexar County, before returning to the legislature in 1891. He died in San Antonio in August, 1892, at age fifty-six.[1]

Jacob Wurzbach died in 1879 in San Antonio. In his will he wrote: "Having provided for my children out of my first marriage by a good education and other help, and started them so far as to enable them to provide for themselves, I therefore give, bequeath and dispose of all that I possess . . . in favor of my wife Josephine and the four children of my second marriage."[2]

While his teen-aged sons, one a Dragoon and the other a Texas

Ranger, back in the 1850s might have disputed the "good education and other help," certainly Jacob had imbued his sons with self-reliance, a lust for adventure, and a cool courage that stood them in good stead in the days of the Texas frontier and during the long trauma of the War of the Rebellion.

Dutch and Matilda settled down in San Antonio to raise a large family of twelve children. Dutch wrote, "After the surrender of General Lee in 1865, I had my honorable discharge sent to me from headquarters."[3] The honorable discharge is dated Richmond, Texas, May 25, 1865.[4]

But for Dutch the war was not yet over. He wrote, "I suffered with my eyes until 1870. I tried doctors from San Antonio to Dallas." At last he found a physician in Dallas County who "cured my eyes in less than six weeks."[5]

Always pithy, Dutch concluded his memoirs by stating, "That is all I can remember of my scouting trips, trips across the Western country, and my war experience, as I am now seventy-eight years old in this year of Our Lord 1915."[6]

For many years, Dutch owned a small horse ranch a few miles outside San Antonio. In middle age he sold the ranch and opened a general store and slaughterhouse in the city. After Matilda died in 1909, he retired and lived with his unmarried daughter, Fanny, in a small house on South Gevers Street, about a mile from his son Levi's house on East Commerce Street.

In later years, according to his granddaughter, Charlotte Wurzbach Brunson, "He was always erect and walked briskly to our house. He had a full head of snow-white, curly hair and a big smile for everyone."[7]

On the warm afternoon of April 8, 1930, after spending the morning frolicking with his great-grandchildren, the author among them, he hiked back to his home and sat in his favorite overstuffed chair, as Fanny brought him a cool glass of lemonade. Relaxed, he closed his eyes and died. He was ninety-two years old.[8]

Earlier, on December 6, 1921, my father and mother were married. In the back yard of the Wurzbach home on East Commerce

Street, they held a reception for family friends and army buddies, who sipped a "fruit" punch that, if subjected to even a cursory analysis, would have shown a fine disregard for both the letter and the spirit of the Volstead Act.

My father's regiment supplied half of the 16th Infantry's band to play fox-trots and the more genteel music of the day. During the wedding festivities, Dutch, then eighty-three years old, took a hearty sampling of the punch and stomped up to my father. "That's a pretty good Yankee band you have there," he said.

My father asked, "Is there anything you would like them to play?"

"Yes," Dutch replied. And, as the grinning sergeant who was leading the group came up, Dutch asked, "Can you play 'The Bonny Blue Flag'?"

"Well, no," the sergeant replied, "I'm afraid we don't know that tune."

Dutch snorted, "Well, then, can you play 'The Robert E. Lee March'?"

The sergeant shook his head: "I'm afraid we don't know that either."

Dutch looked incredulous. "Well, then, play 'The Yellow Rose of Texas,'" he barked.

The sergeant shook his head. "Sorry," he mumbled.

Dutch whipped his old frontiersman's glaring eyes from the abashed sergeant to the trim lieutenant and snapped, "You damn yankees don't know anything." But as he stomped off toward the punch bowl, my father noted a twinkle in his eye and the faint trace of a smile creasing the old man's weathered face.[9]

Notes

CHAPTER 1. ON TO TEXAS

1. Emil Frederick Wurzbach, *Life and Memoirs of Emil Frederick Wurzbach*, 13; Chester W. Geue and Ethel H. Geue, *A New Land Beckoned: German Immigration to Texas, 1844–1847*, 155. Dutch gives the date of the family's arrival in Galveston as Feb. 14, 1844. This date is incorrect. Geue and Geue, 155, prints the passenger manifest of the *Andacia*, showing Jacob Daniel Wurzbach arriving in Galveston on Mar. 29, 1846.
2. Glen E. Lich, *The German Texans*, 28. Lich quotes a letter written by Ottilie Fuchs Goeth in the 1840s.
3. Alwin H. Sörgel, *A Sojourn in Texas, 1846–1847*, xxvii.
4. Ibid., 14–15.
5. Lich, *German Texans*, 29. Lich quotes a letter from Amanda Fallier von Rosenburg, written aboard the *Franziska* during the 1840s.
6. Sörgel, *Sojourn in Texas*, 12.
7. Ibid.
8. Ibid., 14.
9. August Santleben, *A Texas Pioneer: Early Staging and Overland Freighting Days on the Frontiers of Texas and Mexico*, 1.
10. Gilbert Giddings Benjamin, *The Germans in Texas: A Study in Immigration*, 7:49.
11. Paraphrase of a conversation between the author's father,

Vincent D. Meed, and Dutch Wurzbach in San Antonio, Texas, 1921, as reported to the author, Douglas V. Meed, by Vincent D. Meed in Houston, Texas, 1947.

12. Frederick C. Chabot, *With the Makers of San Antonio*, 406.
13. Carl, Prince of Solms-Braunfels, *Texas, 1844–1845*, 1. The quotation comes from a document deposited by Carl in the cornerstone of the Sophienburg, his Texas headquarters at New Braunfels, Texas.
14. Benjamin, *Germans in Texas*, 18.
15. Sörgel, *Sojourn in Texas*, 35.
16. Ibid., 57.
17. Wurzbach, *Life and Memoirs*, 13. Dutch gives the date as 1845, but it must have been 1846.
18. Ibid.
19. Ibid.
20. Sörgel, *Sojourn in Texas*, 80.
21. Ibid., 57.
22. Ferdinand Roemer, *Texas, with Particular Reference to German Immigration and the Physical Appearance of the Country*, 21.
23. Ibid., 21–22.
24. Ibid., 22–23.
25. Sörgel, *Sojourn in Texas*, 62.
26. Wurzbach, *Life and Memoirs*, 13.
27. Sörgel, *Sojourn in Texas*, 87.
28. Ibid.
29. Roemer, *Texas*, 22.
30. Viktor Bracht, *Texas in 1848*, 168.
31. Wurzbach, *Life and Memoirs*, 13.
32. Ibid.
33. Roemer, *Texas*, 92.
34. Geue and Geue, *A New Land Beckoned*, 8.
35. Rosa Kleberg, "Early Experiences in Texas," 2 pts., *Texas Historical Association Quarterly* 1, no. 4 (Apr., 1898): 298, and 2, no. 2 (Oct., 1898): 170.
36. Ibid., 1:297–98, 2:172.
37. Caroline von Hinueber, "Life of German Pioneers in Early Texas," *Texas Historical Association Quarterly* 2 (1899): 227, 229.

38. Henry B. Dielmann, "Emma Altgelt's Sketches of Life in Texas," *Southwestern Historical Quarterly* 63, no. 3 (Jan., 1960): 363, 365.
39. Solms-Braunfels, *Texas, 1844–1845*, 44–45.
40. Ibid., 4.
41. Irene Marschall King, *John O. Meusebach: German Colonizer in Texas*, 58.
42. Ibid., 95.
43. Ibid., 63.
44. Lich, *German Texans*, 47–48.
45. King, *John O. Meusebach*, 75.
46. Roemer, *Texas*, 227–29.
47. Chabot, *With the Makers*, 406.
48. Roemer, *Texas*, 241–42.
49. Ibid., 235, 241.
50. Francis Abernethy, "Texas Folklore and German Culture," in *Texas and Germany: Crosscurrents*, ed. Joseph Wilson, 91. The custom of lighting fires in the hills in remembrance of the treaty is still carried on by the people of Fredericksburg during the Easter season. Robert Penninger, ed., *Fredericksburg, Texas: The First Fifty Years*, 32, 33, 38.
51. Vincent D. Meed, conversation with Douglas V. Meed, Houston, Texas, 1947. Germans often were nicknamed "Dutch" or known as "Dutchies" or "Dutchmen." Such terms probably derived from a corruption of the German word *deutsch*, meaning *German*. It was not a nickname for immigrants from Holland.
52. Lich, *German Texans*, 15; Glen E. Lich, "Goethe on the Guadalupe," *German Culture in Texas: A Free Earth*, ed. Glen E. Lich and Dona B. Reeves, 41.

CHAPTER 2. A-WANDERING

1. Wurzbach, *Life and Memoirs*, 13–14.
2. Ibid.
3. Ibid.
4. Ibid.
5. Kenneth Franklin Neighbors, *Robert Simpson Neighbors and the*

Texas Frontier, 1836–1859. This is the only full-scale biography of one of the state's most outstanding frontiersmen.

6. John Salmon Ford, *Rip Ford's Texas*, ed. Stephen B. Oates, 455.
7. Wurzbach, *Life and Memoirs*, 14; Neighbors, *Robert Simpson Neighbors*, 100.
8. Wurzbach, *Life and Memoirs*, 14.
9. Ibid.
10. Wurzbach, *Life and Memoirs*, 15; Chabot, *With the Makers*, 409.
11. Texas Gov. E. M. Pease to Brig. Gen. P. F. Smith, Sept. 5, 1855, in Dorman H. Winfrey and James M. Day, eds., *The Indian Papers of Texas and the Southwest, 1825–1916*, 3:235.
12. Wurzbach, *Life and Memoirs*, 15.
13. Ibid.
14. W. G. Freeman, "W. G. Freeman's Report on the Eighth Military Department," ed. M. L. Crimmins, 13 parts, *Southwestern Historical Quarterly* 53 (July, 1949–Mar., 1950): pt. 12, 462–65.
15. Sandra L. Myers, "Fort Graham: Listening Post on the Texas Frontier," *West Texas Historical Association Yearbook* 59 (1983): 33–51.
16. Wurzbach, *Life and Memoirs*, 15–16.
17. Ibid., 16.
18. Ibid.
19. Chabot, *With the Makers*, 406.
20. Wurzbach, *Life and Memoirs*, 16.
21. Ibid.
22. Ibid., 17.
23. On "Big Foot" Wallace, see John C. Duval, *The Adventures of Big Foot Wallace;* Walter Prescott Webb, ed., *The Handbook of Texas*, 2:856. On Henry Skillman, see Jerry D. Thompson, "Drama in the Desert: The Hunt for Henry Skillman in the Trans-Pecos, 1862–1864," *Password* (El Paso, Tex.) 37, no. 3 (Fall, 1992): 107–26; Dan L. Thrapp, *Encyclopedia of Western Biography*, 1315–16.
24. Wurzbach, *Life and Memoirs*, 17.
25. Ibid.

26. W. C. Holden, "Frontier Defense, 1846–1860," *West Texas Historical Association Yearbook* 6 (1930): 35–64.
27. Ibid.
28. Records of Charles Wurzbach, Record Group 94, National Archives. A note written by Jacob Wurzbach in English, dated July 23, 1854, reads: "This is to certify that my son Charles Wurzbach has my consent to enlist in the U.S. Army for five years, unless discharged by proper authority."
29. Wurzbach, *Life and Memoirs*, 17; A. J. Sowell, *Early Settlers and Indian Fighters of Southwest Texas*, 353–67.
30. Sowell, *Early Settlers*, 353.
31. Wurzbach, *Life and Memoirs*, 17.
32. Robert J. Casey, *The Texas Border and Some Borderliners*, 126, 136.
33. Wurzbach, *Life and Memoirs*, 17.
34. Ibid; W. G. Freeman, "W. G. Freeman's Report on the Eighth Military Department," ed. M. L. Crimmins, 13 parts, *Southwestern Historical Quarterly* 51 (July, 1947–Mar., 1948): pt. 3, 252.
35. Ibid.
36. Ibid., 255.
37. Ibid., 256, 258.
38. Wurzbach, *Life and Memoirs*, 17.
39. Freeman, "W. G. Freeman's Report," pt. 3, 252; Wurzbach, *Life and Memoirs*, 17. Freeman says the river was 4½ feet deep and 75 feet wide, at the ford nearest the fort.
40. *Colorado Tribune* (Matagorda, Tex.), June 5, 1854; *Northern Standard* (Clarksville, Tex.), June 10, 1854. Both newspapers quoted a long letter by Charles Russell describing the event. There are minor differences in the two accounts. *Northern Standard*'s report conforms more to Dutch's version of events.
41. Foster Harris, *The Look of the Old West*, 162.
42. Wurzbach, *Life and Memoirs*, 18.
43. Chabot, *With the Makers*, 385.
44. Wurzbach, *Life and Memoirs*, 18.
45. *Colorado Tribune* (Matagorda, Tex.), May 22, 1854, p. 2.
46. Wurzbach, *Life and Memoirs*, 18.

47. *Northern Standard* (Clarksville, Tex.), June 10, 1854, p. 2.
48. *Colorado Tribune* (Matagorda, Tex.), June 5, 1854, p. 2.
49. Ibid.
50. Francis A. Lord and Arthur Wise, *Bands and Drummer Boys of the Civil War*, 98, 226, 228. "Boots and Saddles," the U.S. Cavalry bugle call, meant exactly what the title implies: "Put on your boots and saddle your mount." It announced breaking camp and going on a march, or preparing to go into combat. In a quieter time, it was a call for mounted drill. The bugle call is said to be of English origin. In the French cavalry, the call has the same rhythm as the American but begins a fifth note lower, leading one authority to suggest that our version is derived from the French one.
51. *Colorado Tribune*, June 5, 1854, p. 2.
52. Ibid.
53. Albert G. Brackett, *History of the United States Cavalry*, 131.
54. *Colorado Tribune*, July 21, 1854, p. 2.
55. Wurzbach, *Life and Memoirs*, 19.
56. Ibid.

CHAPTER 3. THE TEXAS FRONTIER

1. Wurzbach, *Life and Memoirs*, 19.
2. Ibid.
3. Frank W. Johnson, *A History of Texas and Texans*, 1:511. Johnson quotes U.S. House of Representatives, Committee on Military Affairs, *Report of the U.S. House of Representatives Committee on Military Affairs*, Jan. 17, 1853.
4. *Texas State Gazette* (Austin), July 12, 1851.
5. Wurzbach, *Life and Memoirs*, 17.
6. Holden, "Frontier Defense, 1846–1860," 50.
7. Wurzbach, *Life and Memoirs*, 19.
8. David G. Burnet to H. R. Schoolcraft, Sept. 29, 1847, in Winfrey and Day, *Indian Papers of Texas*, 3:84–99.
9. Ibid., 3:87.
10. Ibid., 3:91–92.
11. Robert S. Neighbors to H. R. Schoolcraft, undated, in Winfrey and Day, *Indian Papers of Texas*, 3:353.

12. Ibid., 3:356.
13. Rupert Norval Richardson, *The Comanche Barrier to South Plains Settlement*, 265.
14. Ibid., 177.
15. John M. Elkins, *Indian Fighting on the Texas Frontier*, 13.
16. Ibid., 15.
17. Wurzbach, *Life and Memoirs*, 19.
18. Neighbors, *Robert Simpson Neighbors*, 132, 150.
19. Clara Lena Koch, "The Federal Indian Policy in Texas, 1845–1860," *Southwestern Historical Quarterly* 29, pt. 1 (Oct., 1925): 98–101.
20. Neighbors, *Robert Simpson Neighbors*, 152.
21. Ibid., 153.
22. Wurzbach, *Life and Memoirs*, 19.
23. Ibid.
24. Ibid.
25. Freeman, "W. G. Freeman's Report," pt. 12, 443.
26. Wurzbach, *Life and Memoirs*, 19.
27. Freeman, "W. G. Freeman's Report," pt. 12, 443.
28. Richard Irving Dodge, *Our Wild Indians: Thirty-Three Years of Personal Experience Among the Red Men of the Great West*, 341–42.
29. Rupert Norval Richardson, *The Frontier of Northwest Texas, 1846–1876*, 97–98.
30. Rupert N. Richardson, B. W. Aston, and Ira Donathan Taylor, *Along Texas Old Forts Trail*, 46–48.
31. Wurzbach, *Life and Memoirs*, 19.
32. Freeman, "W. G. Freeman's Report," pt. 12, 449.
33. C. C. Rister, "The Border Post of Phantom Hill," *West Texas Historical Association Yearbook* 14 (Oct., 1938): 4–7.
34. Eliza Johnston [Mrs. Albert Sidney Johnston], "The Diary of Eliza Johnston: The Second Cavalry Comes to Texas," ed. Charles P. Roland and Richard C. Robbins, *Southwestern Historical Quarterly* 60, no. 4 (Apr., 1957): 483–85.
35. Jodye Lynn Dickson Schilz and Thomas Schilz, *Buffalo Hump and the Penateka Comanches*, 40.
36. Wurzbach, *Life and Memoirs*, 19–20.

CHAPTER 4. MEXICAN ADVENTURE

1. Wurzbach, *Life and Memoirs*, 20.
2. Ibid.
3. Ibid.
4. Ibid.
5. Ibid.
6. Ibid.
7. Ibid., 20, 21.
8. The story of Crabb's expedition is told by the following: Rodolfo F. Acuña, *Sonoran Strongman: Ignacio Pesqueira and His Times;* Thomas Edwin Farish, *History of Arizona;* Robert H. Forbes, *Crabb's Filibustering Expedition.*
9. Wurzbach, *Life and Memoirs*, 20, 21.
10. Ibid. See also n. 8 above. Today, each April, the citizens of Caborca hold a festival, with orators, costumed dancers, and marching bands, celebrating Crabb's defeat.
11. Wurzbach, *Life and Memoirs*, 20, 21. This is another instance of Dutch's confusing phonetic spelling. During the early 1850s, a series of bloody fights occurred between the Mojave and the Yuma (or Quechan) Indians and their hereditary enemies, the Cocopah, Maricopa, and Pima tribes. Dutch must have gotten the date wrong in his memoirs, indicating that he saw the battle in 1856. But the big fight occurred in September, 1857.
12. Clifton B. Kroeber and Bernard L. Fontana, *Massacre on the Gila: An Account of the Last Major Battle Between American Indians, with Reflections on the Origin of War*, 27. This is the most detailed account of the Yuma-Maricopa battle.
13. Ibid., 5, 6.
14. Ibid., 8.
15. Ibid., 19.
16. Ibid., 11, 12.

CHAPTER 5. MINING, MORMONS, AND MATILDA

1. Wurzbach, *Life and Memoirs*, 21.
2. Ibid., 21–22. In his memoirs, Dutch spelled the name *Tumocrockrie.* The two men may not have been as crazy as they

acted. Several Germans had claimed that they bought the mission and the surrounding land. While trying to get their purchase validated, this pair may have put on an act and stayed there to keep rival claimants away.

3. Wurzbach, *Life and Memoirs*, 22. The memoirs spell it *Collibaos*.
4. Ibid. This could be the abandoned mission at La Osa, although this would have meant a major westward detour. Dutch also mentions a Saint Harcova, which the author was unable to identify.
5. Wurzbach, *Life and Memoirs*, 22.
6. Ibid.
7. Ibid., 23.
8. Ibid.
9. Ibid.
10. Ibid.
11. Ibid.
12. Ibid., 23–24.
13. Alvin M. Josephy, Jr., *The Civil War in the American West*, 48.
14. Ibid., 49. The allegations of drunkenness by the Fort Fillmore garrison are also recounted in Martin Hardwick Hall, *Sibley's New Mexico Campaign*.
15. Wurzbach, *Life and Memoirs*, 24.
16. Ibid. In his memoirs, Dutch refers to him as General Harvey.
17. Brackett, *History of the United States Cavalry*, 178–80.
18. Ibid., 178.
19. Wurzbach, *Life and Memoirs*, 24; Charles P. Roland, *Albert Sidney Johnston: Soldier of Three Republics*.
20. Roland, *Albert Sidney Johnston*, 208–10.
21. Wurzbach, *Life and Memoirs*, 24.
22. Brackett, *History of the United States Cavalry*, 179–80.
23. Roland, *Albert Sidney Johnston*, 214.
24. Wurzbach, *Life and Memoirs*, 25.
25. Ibid.
26. Ibid.
27. Ibid.
28. Ibid., 26.

29. Ibid.
30. Ibid., 26–27. In traveling east from Salt Lake City, Dutch and his companions followed the Oregon Trail, which swung north in a semicircle along the route of the present U.S. Highway 80, dipping back south to Fort Laramie. In his memoirs, Fort Laramie is spelled *Ft. Larma* and Fort Caspar is spelled *Ft. Corma.* He also locates Fort Laramie west, instead of east, of Fort Caspar. A little confusion is understandable, with Dutch writing at age seventy-eight and more than fifty years after the events recounted; transcription and typographical errors likely also occurred.
31. Francis Parkman, *The Oregon Trail*, 95.
32. David L. Hieb, *Fort Laramie*, 8.
33. Wurzbach, *Life and Memoirs*, 27.
34. Ibid.
35. Stowe Family Records. This is a handwritten genealogy record tracing the Matilda Stowe family back to 1750 in upper New York State. It was given to the author by his mother, Margo Wurzbach Meed, in San Antonio around 1970. She apparently received it from a member of the Stowe family still residing in San Antonio. Handwritten notes are in possession of the author.

CHAPTER 6. OR FIGHT FOR EVERMORE

1. William W. White, "The Texas Slave Insurrection of 1860," *Southwestern Historical Quarterly* 52, no. 3 (Jan., 1949): 259–85.
2. Roy P. Bosler, ed., *The Collected Works of Abraham Lincoln*, 2:461. The speech was given before the Republican State Convention at Springfield, Ill., on June 16, 1858.
3. Walter L. Buenger, *Secession and the Union in Texas*, 67.
4. Linda Wurzbach, Family Records. Linda Wurzbach of San Antonio is the great-great granddaughter of Dutch. She has compiled and photocopied family records from Bexar County, Texas records consisting of voter registration lists; Texas cemetery records; wills probated in Bexar County; birth certificates; death certificates, and 1800, 1890, and 1900 census reports. Military Service Records of Charles Wurzbach, Texas

Confederate Records, Texas State Archives, Texas State Library, Austin.

5. Wurzbach Family Records, Bexar County death certificate, 1861, in possession of Linda Wurzbach.
6. Military Service Records of Emil F. Wurzbach, Texas Confederate Records, Texas State Archives, Texas State Library, Austin.
7. Wurzbach Family Records, Bexar County birth certificate, 1862, in possession of Linda Wurzbach.
8. Military Service Records of Emil F. Wurzbach, Texas State Archives.
9. Stowe Family Records. This handwritten genealogy record traces the Matilda Stowe family to 1750 in upper New York state. The author received the record from his mother, Margo Wurzbach Meed in San Antonio, circa 1970. She apparently received it from a Stowe family member residing in San Antonio. Where Matilda stayed and how she supported her child while Dutch was gone are not known; however, in addition to her parents, who may have been alive and living in the San Antonio area, family records indicate that she had eight brothers and two sisters, some of whom might have been living nearby. Perhaps she stayed with members of her family or with the Jacob Wurzbach family. Handwritten notes in possession of the author.
10. Alwyn Barr, *Polignac's Texas Brigade*, 4.
11. *Dallas Herald*, Feb. 12, 1862.
12. *Dallas Herald*, Jan. 15, 22, 29; Feb. 5, 12, 1862.
13. Col. George W. Guess to Mrs. Sarah Horton Cockrell, in Monroe F. Cockrell Collection. Photostats of original Civil War letters. Reference is to preface by Monroe F. Cockrell, July 1, 1945, pg. 1; Barr, *Polignac's Texas Brigade*, 5, 10.
14. On uniforms of Texas Confederate troops, see Stephen B. Oates, *Confederate Cavalry West of the River;* Arthur J. Freemantle, *The Freemantle Diary*, 7, 16.
15. Stephen B. Oates, "Recruiting Confederate Cavalry in Texas," *Southwestern Historical Quarterly* 64 (Apr., 1961): 474.
16. *San Antonio Herald*, May 3, 1862.

17. Ibid.
18. Ibid.
19. Wurzbach, *Life and Memoirs*, 27.
20. *San Antonio Herald*, May 3, 1862.
21. Barr, *Polignac's Texas Brigade*, 5.
22. *Dallas Herald*, May 31, 1862.
23. *Dallas Herald*, June 14, 1862.
24. Wurzbach, *Life and Memoirs*, 27.
25. Norman D. Brown, ed., *Journey to Pleasant Hill: The Civil War Letters of Captain Elijah P. Petty, Walker's Texas Division, C.S.A.*, 78–79.
26. Johnette Highsmith Ray, ed., "Civil War Letters from Parson's Texas Cavalry Brigade," *Southwestern Historical Quarterly* 69 (1965): 217–18.
27. Frank E. Vandiver, *Their Tattered Flags*, 189.
28. Vincent D. Meed, conversation with Douglas V. Meed, Houston, Texas, 1947.
29. *Dallas Herald*, July 5, 1862.
30. Guess to Cockrell, June 29, 1862, Guess Civil War Letters.
31. Barr, *Polignac's Texas Brigade*, 5–6.
32. Ibid., 1.
33. Robert S. Weddle, *Plow-Horse Cavalry: The Caney Creek Boys of the Thirty-Fourth Texas*, 34.
34. Barr, *Polignac's Texas Brigade*, 6.
35. Bobby L. Roberts, "General T. C. Hindman and the Trans-Mississippi District," *Arkansas Historical Quarterly* 32 (1973): 301.
36. John N. Edwards, *Shelby and His Men, or, The War in the West*, 87.
37. U.S. War Department, *The War of the Rebellion: A Compilation of the Official Records of the Union and Confederate Armies* (hereafter referred to as *Official Records*), ser. 1, 13:281–82.
38. Ibid., 13:282.
39. Ibid., 13:661–62.
40. Buck Walton, *An Epitome of My Life: Civil War Reminiscences*, 56.
41. Guess to Cockrell, July 17, 1862, Guess Civil War Letters.
42. Edwards, *Shelby and His Men*, 71.
43. Weddle, *Plow-House Cavalry*, 26.

44. Walton, *Epitome of My Life*, 26.
45. *Dallas Herald*, Aug. 18, 1862.
46. *Dallas Herald*, Sept. 6, 1862.
47. Guess to Cockrell, July 29, 1862, Guess Civil War Letters.
48. Ibid.
49. Ibid.
50. Ibid.
51. On the fight at Shirley's Ford, see *Official Records*, ser. 1, 13:277–78; Barr, *Polignac's Texas Brigade*, 6–7.
52. *Dallas Herald*, Oct. 11, 1862.
53. Weddle, *Plow-Horse Cavalry*, 51.
54. *Official Records*, ser. 1, 13:296–300, 13:305–306; Josephy, *Civil War in the West*, 361.
55. Weddle, *Plow-Horse Cavalry*, 53.
56. Walton, *Epitome of My Life*, 49.
57. *Official Records*, ser. 1, 13:288.
58. Ibid., 13:305–306.
59. Ibid., 13:299.
60. Ibid., 13:287–91.
61. Ibid., 13:333–34.
62. Wurzbach, *Life and Memoirs*, 27.
63. *Official Records*, ser. 1, 13:46–50, 13:333–34.
64. Ibid., 13:325–27.
65. Wurzbach, *Life and Memoirs*, 27–28.
66. *Official Records*, ser. 1, 13:48–51.
67. Ibid.
68. Wurzbach, *Life and Memoirs*, 27.
69. *Dallas Herald*, Nov. 22, 1862.
70. Wurzbach, *Life and Memoirs*, 27; for birth of Mary Ann see Wurzbach Family Records, Bexar County, Texas birth record, in possession of Linda Wurzbach.
71. Josephy, *Civil War in the West*, 366.
72. *Official Records*, ser. 1, 13:299.
73. Barr, *Polignac's Texas Brigade*, 11.
74. Mark Mayo Boatner, III, *The Civil War Dictionary*, 95.
75. A. L. Nelms to M. J. Nelms, Dec. 24, 1862, in Montee Nelms Weddle Collection; Weddle, *Plow-Horse Cavalry*, 85.

76. *Dallas Herald*, Oct. 4, 1862.
77. Barr, *Polignac's Texas Brigade*, 11.
78. Ibid., 15.
79. Guess to Cockrell, Mar. 6, 1863, Guess Civil War Letters.
80. *Dallas Herald*, Feb. 11, 1863.
81. *Official Records*, ser. 1, pt. 1, 22:28–29.
82. Ibid.
83. Weddle, *Plow-Horse Cavalry*, 96.
84. Marcus J. Wright, *Texas in the War, 1861–1865*, 18.
85. *Official Records*, ser. 1, pt. 1, 22:28–29.
86. *Official Records*, ser. 1, pt. 2, 22:776–79.
87. Ibid., 794–95.
88. William E. Sawyer and Neal A. Baker, Jr., eds., "A Texan in the Civil War," *Texas Military History* 2, no. 4 (Nov., 1962): 275.
89. John Q. Anderson, *A Texas Surgeon in the C.S.A.*, 40.
90. Barr, *Polignac's Texas Brigade*, 15; Weddle, *Plow-Horse Cavalry*, 88.
91. Sawyer and Baker, "Texan in the Civil War," 276.
92. Barr, *Polignac's Texas Brigade*, 16.
93. J. P. Blessington, *The Campaigns of Walker's Texas Division*, 68.
94. Guess to Cockrell, Dec. 16, 1862, Guess Civil War Letters.
95. Ray, "Civil War Letters from Parson's Texas Cavalry Brigade," 219.
96. On the effects of dismounting Texas cavalry and turning them into infantry, see *Official Records*, ser. 1, pt. 2, 26:278–79.
97. *Official Records*, ser. 1, pt. 2, 22:796–97.

CHAPTER 7. BATTLES IN THE BAYOUS

1. Weddle, *Plow-Horse Cavalry*, 88.
2. Guess to Cockrell, Mar. 6, 1863, Guess Civil War Letters.
3. Barr, *Polignac's Texas Brigade*, 17.
4. *Official Records*, ser. 1, pt. 2, 22:805.
5. Ibid., 802.
6. Ibid.
7. Ibid., 803.
8. Guess to Cockrell, May 5, 1863, Guess Civil War Letters.
9. *Dallas Herald*, May 13 and 27, 1863.

10. *Official Records*, ser. 1, pt. 2, 22:839–40.
11. Barr, *Polignac's Texas Brigade*, 19.
12. *Official Records*, ser. 1, pt. 1, 26:6.
13. Barr, *Polignac's Texas Brigade*, 19.
14. Richard Taylor, *Destruction and Reconstruction*, 122.
15. B. P. Gallaway, *The Ragged Rebel: A Common Soldier in W. H. Parsons' Texas Cavalry, 1861–1865*, 72.
16. Walton, *Epitome of My Life*, 73–74.
17. John D. Winters, *The Civil War in Louisiana*, 262.
18. Blessington, *Campaigns of Walker's Texas Division*, 93.
19. Sawyer and Baker, "Texan in the Civil War," 277.
20. Barr, *Polignac's Texas Brigade*, 19.
21. Emil Frederick Wurzbach, *Life and Memoirs*, 28.
22. Barr, *Polignac's Texas Brigade*, 20; T. Michael Parrish, *Richard Taylor: Soldier Prince of Dixie*, 252–53.
23. Anderson, *Texas Surgeon*, 67–68.
24. Blessington, *Campaigns of Walker's Texas Division*, 124.
25. Barr, *Polignac's Texas Brigade*, 22.
26. *Dallas Herald*, Nov. 22, 1862; Aug. 19, 1863.
27. Guess to Cockrell, Aug. 22 and Sept. 9, 1863, Guess Civil War Letters.
28. Barr, *Polignac's Texas Brigade*, 23.
29. Ibid.
30. *Official Records*, ser. 1, pt. 1, 26:329–32; Barr, *Polignac's Texas Brigade*, 25.
31. George W. O'Brien, "The Diary of Captain George W. O'Brien, 1863," *Southwestern Historical Quarterly* 67, pt. 2 (Oct., 1963): 237.
32. Ibid., 245.
33. Walter Prescott Webb, *The Texas Rangers: A Century of Frontier Defense*, 454.
34. James E. Harrison to William Pitt Ballinger, Oct. 8, 1863, William Pitt Ballinger Collection. This collection includes thirty letters from Harrison to Ballinger.
35. *Official Records*, ser. 1, pt. 1, 26:329–32.
36. Ibid.
37. On the Battle of Stirling Plantation (Battle of Bayou

Fordoche), see *Official Records*, ser. 1, pt. 1, 26:329–32; Barr, *Polignac's Texas Brigade*, 24–27; Winters, *Civil War in Louisiana*, 296–97; O'Brien, "Diary of Captain George W. O'Brien," pt. 2, 235–45.

38. Guess to Cockrell, Sept. 9, 15, and 22, 1863, Guess Civil War Letters.
39. Ludwell H. Johnson, *Red River Campaign: Politics and Cotton in the Civil War*, 47.
40. Guess to Cockrell, July 4, 1864, Guess Civil War Letters.
41. Guess to Cockrell, Sept. 22, 1863, Guess Civil War Letters.
42. *Official Records*, ser. 1, pt. 1, 26:322–24.
43. Barr, *Polignac's Texas Brigade*, 5.
44. Roy O. Hatton, "Prince Camille de Polignac and the American Civil War, 1863–1865," *Louisiana Studies* 3 (Summer, 1964):163–68.
45. Ibid., 167.
46. Taylor, *Destruction and Reconstruction*, 150–51.
47. D. D. Whetston, "Book of Adventures," Oct. 20, 1863, typescript, 144. This typescript probably was created from hand-scrawled notes. The page numbers and dates are those used in the typescript; Barr, *Polignac's Texas Brigade*, 29.
48. Ibid.
49. Blessington, *Campaigns of Walker's Texas Division*, 133.
50. *Official Records*, ser. 1, pt. 1, 26:356; Whetston, "Book of Adventures," 144. Whetston reported that a trooper was sent as far as San Antonio to try to get clothing for the ragged regiment.
51. Silas T. Grisamore, *Civil War Reminiscences*, ed. Arthur W. Bergeron, Jr., 130.
52. Whetston, "Book of Adventures," 41.
53. Ibid., 100.
54. O'Brien, "Diary of Captain George W. O'Brien," pt. 3, 426–27.
55. Blessington, *Campaigns of Walker's Texas Division*, 153.
56. Ibid., 163.
57. Whetston, "Book of Adventures," 100.
58. O'Brien, "Diary of Captain George W. O'Brien," pt. 3, 433.

59. Gallaway, *Ragged Rebel*, 77.
60. Blessington, *Campaigns of Walker's Texas Division*, 159.
61. Ibid., 160–61.
62. Winters, *Civil War in Louisiana*, 322–23.
63. Whetston, "Book of Adventures," 116, 118.
64. Hatton, "Prince Camille de Polignac," 169.
65. Ibid.
66. Weddle, *Plow-Horse Cavalry*, 96.
67. Whetston, "Book of Adventures," 124.
68. Ibid.
69. *Official Records*, ser. 1, pt. 2, 34:977.
70. H. Allen Gosnell, *Guns on the Western Waters: The Story of River Gunboats in the Civil War*, 5–8.
71. Ibid., 9, 11, 15.
72. Ibid., 3; illustration following 142; 250.
73. Ibid., 19.
74. *Official Records*, ser. 1, pt. 1, 34:155.
75. Ibid.
76. Ibid.
77. *Official Records of the Union and Confederate Navies in the War of the Rebellion*, ser. 1, 25:787–89.
78. Ibid.
79. Taylor, *Destruction and Reconstruction*, 151.

CHAPTER 8. THE RED RIVER CAMPAIGN

1. Johnson, *Red River Campaign*, 35.
2. Shelby Foote, *The Civil War: A Narrative: Red River to Appomattox*, 33.
3. *Official Records*, ser. 1, pt. 1, 36:179–80.
4. Carl Sandburg, *Abraham Lincoln: The War Years*, 3:13.
5. Taylor, *Destruction and Reconstruction*, 160.
6. Johnson, *Red River Campaign*, 107.
7. U.S. Congress, Joint Committee on the Conduct of the War, *Report of the Joint Committee on the Conduct of the War*, vol. 2: *Red River Expedition*, 38th Congress, 2d sess., p. 11.
8. Blessington, *Campaigns of Walker's Texas Division*, 175.
9. Ibid., 183.

10. Brown, *Journey to Pleasant Hill*, 386.
11. Hatton, "Prince Camille de Polignac," 174.
12. Taylor, *Destruction and Reconstruction*, 159.
13. Ibid., 159–60.
14. Blessington, *Campaigns of Walker's Texas Division*, 184.
15. Parrish, *Richard Taylor*, 344.
16. Vincent D. Meed, conversation with Douglas V. Meed in Houston, Texas, 1947. Vincent Meed was reporting a conversation with Dutch in 1921; Blessington, *Campaigns of Walker's Texas Division*, 198, has Polignac shouting, "My boys, follow your Polignac," at the Battle of Pleasant Hill on the following day.
17. Blessington, *Campaigns of Walker's Texas Division*, 188.
18. *Official Records*, pt. 1, 34:564.
19. Parrish, *Richard Taylor*, 346.
20. Johnson, *Red River Campaign*, 137.
21. Taylor, *Destruction and Reconstruction*, 164.
22. Hatton, "Prince Camille de Polignac," 174.
23. Blessington, *Campaigns of Walker's Texas Division*, 193–94.
24. Brown, *Journey to Pleasant Hill*, 253; Gallaway, *Ragged Rebel*, 85.
25. Hatton, "Prince Camille de Polignac," 175.
26. Brown, *Journey to Pleasant Hill*, 412.
27. Parrish, *Richard Taylor*, 365.
28. Blessington, *Campaigns of Walker's Texas Division*, 201.
29. Johnson, *Red River Campaign*, 214.
30. Ibid., 211.
31. Josephy, *Civil War in the West*, 215–16.
32. Foote, *The Civil War*, 57.
33. Ibid., 60.
34. Taylor, *Destruction and Reconstruction*, 189.
35. Wurzbach, *Life and Memoirs*, 28. Dutch refers to this battle as Fort Dora Bayou, a name I have not been able to find on any map or narrative of battle. He says that his regiment was trying to cut the Federals off from the Mississippi River. Most likely this was part of the battle at Yellow Bayou, near Simmesport, fought on May 18, in which Polignac's men attempted to keep

the retreating Union forces from reaching the Atchafalaya River near its junction with the Mississippi. The fight, overall, was a failure, and the Union forces made a successful withdrawal.

36. Taylor, *Destruction and Reconstruction*, 189.
37. Ibid., 192.
38. Ibid., 188.
39. Hatton, "Prince Camille de Polignac," 183–84.
40. Johnson, *Red River Campaign*, 283.
41. Ibid., 284.
42. Wurzbach, *Life and Memoirs*, 28.
43. Guess to Cockrell, July 29, 1862, Guess Civil War Letters.
44. Ralph A. Wooster and Robert Wooster, "'Rarin' for a Fight': Texans in the Confederate Army," *Southwestern Historical Quarterly* 84 (1981): 425.
45. Wurzbach, *Life and Memoirs*, 28.

EPILOGUE

1. Webb, *Handbook of Texas*, 2:939.
2. Jacob D. Wurzbach, Last Will and Testament, filed July 28, 1882, in Probate Court, Bexar County, San Antonio, Tex., provided by Linda Wurzbach.
3. Wurzbach, *Life and Memoirs*, 29.
4. Honorable discharge of Emil Frederick Wurzbach. Texas Confederate Records, Texas State Archives, Texas State Library, Austin.
5. Wurzbach, *Life and Memoirs*, 29.
6. Ibid.
7. Charlotte Wurzbach Brunson, interview by the author at her San Antonio home in summer, 1993. Handwritten notes.
8. Vincent D. Meed, conversation with Douglas V. Meed in Houston, Tex., 1947, and *San Antonio Light*, Apr. 9, 1930.
9. Vincent D. Meed, conversation with Douglas V. Meed in Houston, Tex., 1947.

Bibliography

ARCHIVAL MATERIAL

Ballinger, William Pitt, Collection. Archives. Center for American History, University of Texas, Austin.

Guess, George W. Civil War Letters of Col. George W. Guess to Mrs. Sarah Horton.

Cockrell. Preface by Monroe F. Cockrell. Monroe F. Cockrell Collection. Archives. Center for American History, University of Texas, Austin.

Weddle, Robert S., Collection. Archives. Center for American History, University of Texas, Austin.

Whetston, D. D. "Book of Adventures." Typescript. Archives. Center for American History, University of Texas, Austin.

INTERVIEWS AND FAMILY RECORDS

Brunson, Charlotte Wurzbach. Remembrances. Interview by author. Handwritten notes. San Antonio, Tex., summer, 1993.

Meed, Vincent D. Conversations with Douglas V. Meed. Houston, Tex., spring, 1947.

Stowe Family Records. Handwritten genealogy record of Matilda Stowe family, in possession of the author.

Wurzbach Family Records, in possession of Linda Wurzbach. San Antonio, Texas.

Wurzbach, Jacob D. Last Will and Testament, filed July 28, 1882, in Probate Court, San Antonio, Bexar County, Texas. Photocopy provided by Linda Wurzbach.

GOVERNMENT DOCUMENTS

Muster Roll of Company "C," 31st Texas Cavalry Regiment. April 21, 1862. Texas Confederate Records. Texas Archives, Texas State Library, Austin, Texas.

Muster Roll of Mounted (Texas) Rangers. P. H. Rogers, Captain. December 22, 1854. Texas Archives, Texas State Library, Austin, Texas.

Muster Roll of Van Dorn Mounted Rifles, 30th Brigade. April 21, 1862. Texas Confederate Records. Texas Archives, Texas State Library, Austin, Texas.

Official Records of the Union and Confederate Navies in the War of the Rebellion. Washington, D.C.: U.S. Government Printing Office, 1912.

U.S. Congress. Joint Committee on the Conduct of the War. *Report of the Joint Committee on the Conduct of the War.* Vol. 2: *Red River Expedition.* 38th Congress, 2d sess., 1865.

U.S. War Department. *War of the Rebellion: A Compilation of the Official Records of the Union and Confederate Armies.* Washington, D.C.: U.S. Government Printing Office, 1880–1901.

Wurzbach, Charles. Military Service Records. Texas Confederate Records. Texas Archives, Texas State Library, Austin, Texas.

Wurzbach, Charles. Records. July 23, 1854. Record Group 94. National Archives. Record of enlistment and statement by Jacob Wurzbach.

Wurzbach, Emil F. Military Service Records. Texas Confederate Records. Texas Archives, Texas State Library, Austin, Texas.

BOOKS AND ARTICLES

Abernethy, Francis. "Texas Folklore and German Culture." In *Texas and Germany: Crosscurrents.* Edited by Joseph Wilson. Rice University Studies 63. Houston: Rice University Press, 1977.

Acuña, Rodolfo F. *Sonoran Strongman: Ignacio Pesqueira and His Times.* Tucson: University of Arizona Press, 1974.

Anderson, John Q. *A Texas Surgeon in the C.S.A.* Tuscaloosa, Ala.: Confederate Publishing Company, 1957.

Barr, Alwyn. *Polignac's Texas Brigade.* Volume 8, no. 1. Houston: Texas Gulf Coast Historical Association, 1964.

Benjamin, Gilbert Giddings. *The Germans in Texas: A Study in Immigration.* Philadelphia: University of Pennsylvania, 1909. Reprinted from *German American Annals.* Volume 7.

Blessington, J. P. *The Campaigns of Walker's Texas Division.* New York: Lange, Little and Company, 1875.

Boatner, Mark Mayo, III. *The Civil War Dictionary.* New York: David McKay Company, 1959.

Bosler, Roy P., ed. *The Collected Works of Abraham Lincoln.* Volume 2. New Brunswick, N.J.: Rutgers University Press, 1953.

Bracht, Viktor. *Texas in 1848.* San Antonio: Naylor Printing Co., 1931.

Brackett, Albert G. *History of the United States Cavalry.* 1865. Reprint, New York: Greenwood Press, 1968.

Brown, Norman D., ed. *Journey to Pleasant Hill: The Civil War Letters of Captain Elijah P. Petty, Walker's Texas Division, C.S.A.* San Antonio: Institute of Texan Cultures, University of Texas, 1982.

Buenger, Walter L. *Secession and the Union in Texas.* Austin: University of Texas Press, 1984.

Casey, Robert J. *The Texas Border and Some Borderliners.* New York: Bobbs-Merrill Company, 1950.

Chabot, Frederick C. *With the Makers of San Antonio.* San Antonio: Frederick C. Chabot, 1937.

Dielmann, Henry B. "Emma Altgelt's Sketches of Life in Texas." *Southwestern Historical Quarterly* 63, no. 3 (Jan., 1960): 363–84.

Dodge, Richard Irving. *Our Wild Indians: Thirty-Three Years of Personal Experience Among the Red Men of the Great West.* 1882. Reprint, New York: Archer House, 1959.

Duval, John C. *The Adventures of Big Foot Wallace.* Lincoln: University of Nebraska Press, 1966.

Edwards, John N. *Shelby and His Men, or, The War in the West.* Kansas City, Mo.: Hudson-Kimberly Publishing Company, 1897.

Elkins, John M. *Indian Fighting on the Texas Frontier.* Amarillo, Tex.: Russell and Cockrell, 1929.

Farish, Thomas Edwin. *History of Arizona.* Volume 1. Phoenix, Ariz.: Filmer Brothers, 1915.

Foote, Shelby. *The Civil War: A Narrative: Red River to Appomattox.* Volume 3. New York: Random House, 1974.

Forbes, Robert H. *Crabb's Filibustering Expedition.* Tucson, Ariz.: Arizona Silhouettes, 1952.

Ford, John Salmon. *Rip Ford's Texas.* Edited by Stephen B. Oates. Austin: University of Texas Press, 1963.

Freeman, W. G. "W. G. Freeman's Report on the Eighth Military Department." Edited by M. L. Crimmins. 13 parts. *Southwestern Historical Quarterly* 51 (July, 1947–Mar., 1948): pt. 1, 54–58; pt. 2, 167–74; pt. 3, 252–58; pt. 4, 350–57; 52 (July, 1948–Mar., 1949): pt. 5, 100–108; pt. 6, 227–33; pt. 7, 349–53; pt. 8, 444–47; 53 (July, 1949–Mar., 1950): pt. 9, 71–77; pt. 10, 202–208; pt. 11, 308–19; pt. 12, 443–473; and 54 (July, 1950–Apr., 1951): pt. 13, 202–18.

Freemantle, James A. L. *The Freemantle Diary.* Edited by Walter Lord. Reprint, Boston: Little Brown, 1956.

Gallaway, B. P. *The Ragged Rebel: A Common Soldier in W. H. Parsons' Texas Cavalry, 1861–1865.* Austin: University of Texas Press, 1988.

Geue, Chester W., and Ethel H. Geue. *A New Land Beckoned: German Immigration to Texas, 1844–1847.* Baltimore: Genealogical Publishing Company, 1982.

Gosnell, H. Allen. *Guns on the Western Waters: The Story of River Gunboats in the Civil War.* Baton Rouge: Louisiana State University Press, 1949.

Grisamore, Silas T. *Civil War Reminiscences.* Edited by Arthur W. Bergeron. Baton Rouge: Louisiana State University Press, 1993.

Hall, Martin Hardwick. *Sibley's New Mexico Campaign.* Austin: University of Texas Press, 1960.

Harris, Foster. *The Look of the Old West.* New York: Macmillan, 1955.

Hatton, Roy O. "Prince Camille de Polignac and the American

Civil War, 1863–1865." *Louisiana Studies* 3 (Summer, 1964):163–95.

Hieb, David L. *Fort Laramie.* National Park Service Historical Handbook Series, no. 20. Washington, D.C.: Government Printing Office, 1954.

Holden, W. C. "Frontier Defense, 1846–1860." *West Texas Historical Association Yearbook* 6 (1930): 35–64.

Johnson, Frank W. *A History of Texas and Texans.* Volume 1. Chicago and New York: American Historical Society, 1914.

Johnson, Ludwell H. *Red River Campaign: Politics and Cotton in the Civil War.* Baltimore, Md.: Johns Hopkins University Press, 1958.

Johnston, Eliza [Mrs. Albert Sidney Johnston]. "The Diary of Eliza Johnston: The Second Cavalry Comes to Texas." Edited by Charles P. Roland and Richard C. Robbins. *Southwestern Historical Quarterly* 60, no. 4 (Apr., 1957): 463–500.

Josephy, Alvin M., Jr. *The Civil War in the American West.* New York: Alfred A. Knopf, 1991.

King, Irene Marschall. *John O. Meusebach: German Colonizer in Texas.* Austin: University of Texas Press, 1967.

Kleberg, Rosa. "Early Experiences in Texas." 2 parts. *Texas Historical Association Quarterly* 1, no. 4 (Apr., 1898): 297–302; and 2, no. 2 (Oct., 1898): 170–73.

Koch, Clara Lena. "The Federal Indian Policy in Texas, 1845–1860." 4 parts. *Southwestern Historical Quarterly* 1, vol. 28 (Jan., 1925): 223–34; 2, vol. 28 (Apr., 1925): 259–86; 3, vol. 29 (July, 1925): 19–35; and 4, vol. 29 (Oct., 1925): 98–127.

Kroeber, Clifton B., and Bernard L. Fontana. *Massacre on the Gila: An Account of the Last Major Battle Between American Indians, with Reflections on the Origin of War.* Tucson: University of Arizona Press, 1986.

Lich, Glen E. "Goethe on the Guadalupe." In *German Culture in Texas: A Free Earth.* Edited by Glen E. Lich and Dona B. Reeves. Boston: Twayne, 1980.

———. *The German Texans.* San Antonio: Institute of Texan Cultures, University of Texas, 1981.

Lord, Francis A., and Arthur Wise. *Bands and Drummer Boys of the Civil War.* New York and London: Thomas Yoseloff, Ltd., 1966.

Myers, Sandra L. "Fort Graham: Listening Post on the Texas Frontier." *West Texas Historical Association Yearbook* 59 (1983): 33–51.

Neighbors, Kenneth Franklin. "Robert S. Neighbors in Texas." Ph.D. diss. University of Texas, Austin, 1975.

———. *Robert Simpson Neighbors and the Texas Frontier, 1836–1859.* Waco, Tex.: Texian Press, 1975.

Oates, Stephen B. *Confederate Cavalry West of the River.* Austin: University of Texas Press, 1961.

———. "Recruiting Confederate Cavalry in Texas." *Southwestern Historical Quarterly* 64 (Apr., 1961): 463–77.

O'Brien, George W. "The Diary of Captain George W. O'Brien, 1863." 3 parts. *Southwestern Historical Quarterly* 67, pt. 1 (July, 1963): 26–54; pt. 2 (Oct., 1963): 235–45; pt. 3 (Jan., 1964): 413–33.

Parkman, Francis. *The Oregon Trail.* New York: Modern Library, 1949.

Parrish, T. Michael. *Richard Taylor: Soldier Prince of Dixie.* Chapel Hill: University of North Carolina Press, 1992.

Penninger, Robert, ed. *Fredericksburg, Texas: The First Fifty Years.* Fredericksburg, Tex.: Fredericksburg Publishing Company, 1971.

Ray, Johnette Highsmith, ed. "Civil War Letters from Parson's Texas Cavalry Brigade." *Southwestern Historical Quarterly* 69 (1965): 210–23.

Richardson, Rupert Norval. *The Comanche Barrier to South Plains Settlement.* Glendale, Calif.: Arthur H. Clark Company, 1933.

———. *The Frontier of Northwest Texas, 1846–1876.* Glendale, Calif.: Arthur H. Clark Company, 1963.

Richardson, Rupert N.; B. W. Aston; and Ira Donathan Taylor. *Along Texas Old Forts Trail.* Denton: University of North Texas Press, 1990.

Rister, C. C. "The Border Post of Phantom Hill." *West Texas Historical Association Yearbook* 14 (Oct., 1938): 3–13.

Roberts, Bobby L. "General T. C. Hindman and the Trans-Mississippi District." *Arkansas Historical Quarterly* 32 (1973): 297–311.

Roemer, Ferdinand. *Texas, with Particular Reference to German*

Immigration and the Physical Appearance of the Country. San Antonio: Standard Printing Company, 1935.

Roland, Charles P. *Albert Sidney Johnston: Soldier of Three Republics*. Austin: University of Texas Press, 1964.

Sandburg, Carl. *Abraham Lincoln: The War Years*. Volume 3. New York: Harcourt, Brace and Company, 1939.

Santleben, August. *A Texas Pioneer: Early Staging and Overland Freighting Days on the Frontiers of Texas and Mexico*. New York and Washington, D.C.: Neale Publishing Company, 1910.

Sawyer, William E., and Neal A. Baker, Jr., eds. "A Texan in the Civil War." *Texas Military History* 2, no. 4 (Nov., 1962): 275–78.

Schilz, Jodye Lynn Dickson, and Thomas Schilz. *Buffalo Hump and the Penateka Comanches*. Southwestern Studies, no. 88. El Paso: University of Texas at El Paso, 1989.

Solms-Braunfels, Carl, Prince of. *Texas, 1844–1845*. Houston: Anson Jones Press, 1936.

Sörgel, Alwin H. *A Sojourn in Texas, 1846–1847*. San Marcos, Tex.: German-Texan Heritage Society, Southwest Texas State University, 1992.

Sowell, A. J. *Early Settlers and Indian Fighters of Southwest Texas*. New York: Argosy-Antiquarian, Ltd., 1900.

Taylor, Richard. *Destruction and Reconstruction*. 1879. Reprint, Waltham, Mass.: Blaisdell Publishing Company, 1968.

Thompson, Jerry D. "Drama in the Desert: The Hunt for Henry Skillman in the Trans-Pecos, 1862–1864." *Password* (El Paso, Texas) 37, no. 3 (Fall, 1992): 107–26.

Thrapp, Dan L. *Encyclopedia of Western Biography*. Glendale, Calif.: Arthur H. Clark Company, 1988.

Vandiver, Frank E. *Their Tattered Flags*. New York: Harpers Magazine Press, 1970. Reprint, College Station: Texas A&M University Press, 1987.

von Hinueber, Caroline. "Life of German Pioneers in Early Texas." *Texas Historical Association Yearbook* 2 (1899): 227–32.

Walton, Buck. *An Epitome of My Life: Civil War Reminiscences*. Austin: Waterloo Press, 1965.

Webb, Walter Prescott, ed. *The Handbook of Texas*. Austin: Texas State Historical Association, 1952.

———. *The Texas Rangers: A Century of Frontier Defense.* 1935. Reprint, Austin: University of Texas Press, 1965.

Weddle, Robert S. *Plow-Horse Cavalry: The Caney Creek Boys of the Thirty-Fourth Texas.* Austin: Madrona Press, 1974.

White, William W. "The Texas Slave Insurrection of 1860." *Southwestern Historical Quarterly* 52, no. 3 (Jan., 1949): 259–85.

Winfrey, Dorman H., and James M. Day, eds., *The Indian Papers of Texas and the Southwest, 1825–1916.* Volume 3. Austin: Pemberton Press, 1966.

Winters, John D. *The Civil War in Louisiana.* Baton Rouge: Louisiana State University Press, 1963.

Wooster, Ralph A., and Robert Wooster. "'Rarin' for a Fight': Texans in the Confederate Army." *Southwestern Historical Quarterly* 84 (1981): 387–426.

Wright, Marcus J. *Texas in the War, 1861–1865.* Hillsboro, Tex.: Hill Junior College Press, 1965.

Wurzbach, Emil Frederick. *Life and Memoirs of Emil Frederick Wurzbach.* San Antonio, Tex.: Yanaguana Society, 1937.

Index

Note: Pages with illustrations are indicated by italics.